Free Stuff
FOR
Sewing
Fanatics
ON THE
INTERNET

Judy Heim and Gloria Hansen

Copyright © 1999 Judy Heim and Gloria Hansen
Developmental Editor: Vera Tobin
Technical Editor: Barbara Konzak Kuhn
Cover and Book Design: Christina Jarumay
Book Production: Aliza Kahn
Front Cover Illustration: Alan McCorkle © C&T Publishing, Inc.

Library of Congress Cataloging-in-Publication Data

Heim, Judy.
  Free stuff for sewing fanatics on the Internet / Judy Heim and
Gloria Hansen.
    p. cm.
  Includes index.
  ISBN 1-57120-073-8 (paper trade)
  1. Sewing—Computer network resources Directories. 2. Internet
addresses Directories. 3. Web sites Directories. 4. Free
material—Computer network resources Directories. I. Hansen,
Gloria. II. Title.
  TT715 .H44 1999
  025.06′6462—dc21
                        99-6671
                        CIP

Published by C&T Publishing, Inc.
P.O. Box 1456
Lafayette, California 94549

Printed in Hong Kong
10 9 8 7 6 5 4 3 2 1

Dedication

We dedicate this book to the spirit that inspires sewers and other craftspeople to share so freely of themselves, their skills, and their friendship on the Web. By sharing, we open new worlds in the hearts and minds of others, including strangers we many never meet. We also grow friendships that are irreplaceable—well, like our own!

Judy & Gloria

We hope *Free Stuff for Sewing Fanatics on the Internet* will get you started exploring and enjoying the Web as many sewers are doing already. There are thousands of Web sites about sewing, and the number grows daily. We could not include them all in this book, although we would have liked to. We sifted and sorted and came up with those we think offer valuable information to sewers. That doesn't mean there aren't many others out there that are equally illuminating and valuable. Also, because of the fluid nature of the Internet, it is inevitable that some of the Web sites listed may move or even vanish. Had we included only Web sites that are certain to be around many moons from now, this book wouldn't be nearly as valuable.

Symbols in this book

 You can find lots of free goodies on the Web, but you'll learn more if you follow this sewing bee and join in the many discussion groups offered on the Internet.

 This icon signifies a bit of Judy-and-Gloria hard-earned wisdom—in other words, something we wished we knew when we first started cruising the Web.

 When you see this icon, read carefully—you're about to get a piece of information that will keep you on track.

 This icon means that the Web site also sells products that relate to the information on their site.

Table of Contents

why your Computer May Be Your Best Sewing Buddy

The great news for sewers on the Internet is that you can find directions for sewing just about anything you've ever dreamed of sewing, but were always reluctant to try. For many of us, if something isn't in a pattern book we're afraid to try sewing it. There are many things we'd love to sew: coats, drapes, dolls with needle-sculpted faces. But the prospect of even trying is daunting in itself.

Now you can chat on the Net with sewers who are more than generous in offering their advice and expertise. In fact, we think that this is one of the most amazing things about the Net: so many of us find ourselves trying new methods and embarking on projects we never would have dreamed of in our "pre-cyber" days.

Thinking of starting a sewing business? You'll find discussion groups and Web sites that will help you.

Having problems with your sewing or embroidery machine? Cyberspace teems with dozens of discussion groups devoted to solving the woes of specific brands and models of machine.

Does your daughter want you to sew her a bridal gown like the kind Grace Kelly wore? You can find bridal patterns from just about any period in history on the Web.

Like to learn to tailor clothes that fit you better? You can learn on the Web.

Or maybe you'd like to sew yourself a bra that really fits. Hey, we've got a whole chapter of Web sites that will help you.

The Internet is revolutionizing sewing, bringing people together from every corner of the planet to share ideas, tips, and a sense of community. Whatever you want to sew, you'll find a wealth of information on the Net—so much, in fact, that it can be a little overwhelming.

◆◣ THIS BOOK WILL GET YOU TO WHAT YOU'RE LOOKING FOR FASTER THAN ANYTHING ELSE WILL

"Hey, I can find all that stuff with a Web searcher like Yahoo," you may be scoffing. "Why do I need this book?"

Because the Web is growing as quickly as the universe.

Sure, you could find some of these sites yourself through a Web searcher—if you searched long enough, and visited lots of dumb Web sites in the process. And even if you spend hours on the Web, you still won't find all these goodies, because free stuff is just getting harder to find.

We've sifted through enough Web sites to make our eyes bleary and picked out the ones we think will be valuable to you. We've also tried to select sites that have a history of longevity—in other words, they're not likely to disappear tomorrow. We hate it as much as you do when we pick up an Internet guide and all of the Web addresses are out-of-date.

Finally, it's just handy to have directions to get to the sewing help you need in a little book by your computer—or your sewing machine.

◆◣ IF YOU'VE NEVER BEEN ONLINE BEFORE, TRY AMERICA ONLINE

The easiest way to get on the Net is to pop one of the free startup diskettes from **America Online** (**http://www.aol.com**) into your computer's disk drive. You can get a startup disk by calling 800/827-6364, or have a friend download the software for you from the Web.

Once you've installed the software and have connected to America Online, press Ctrl-K, or Command-K on a Mac, and type the keyword **internet<enter>** or **web<enter>**, and you're on the Internet.

The disadvantages of AOL include hourly fees to access some areas of service and the fact that the closest access number may be a long-distance call for you. Also, AOL's numbers are some-times busy in the evening. AOL also charges additional hourly access fees for anyone connecting from outside the continental United States or anyone calling through an AOL 800 number.

You can get to the sewing forum on America Online by typing the keyword sewing in the address bar. You'll find discussion groups for sewers, files with sewing information, and even patterns. But you must be on AOL to access these things. You can't get to them from the Web.

◆ FOR THE CHEAPEST INTERNET ACCESS, HUNT FOR A LOCAL INTERNET SERVICE

Many people graduate from AOL to an Internet service provider (ISP) with local access numbers. Whether you sign up with a national ISP like **Earthlink (http://www.earthlink.net)** or a local one, shop for one with a fast connection of T1 or better directly into the Internet's network backbone and 56K bps connections that support the same connection standard as your modem does. Ask if telephone support is available in the evening and whether the service offers online help documents. Ask friends and neighbors for recommendations (you don't want an ISP with frequent busy signals or one that's slow at delivering e-mail), or visit **TheList (http://www.thelist.com)**. Most ISPs offer unlimited Internet access for $20/month. That usually includes the ability to set up a Web site.

Connect to America Online
Through Your Internet Service Provider
You probably connect to America Online by calling a local phone number. But you can also tap in through your Internet service provider if you have one. Maybe AOL's phone number is

a long-distance call for you. Or maybe you access the Internet through cable or satellite. AOL's normal rates still apply when you tap in this way, but if you normally pay long-distance rates to get on AOL, this is a good way to avoid them.

In America Online 4.0, on the Signon screen click the Setup button. Select "Create a location for use with new access phone numbers or an ISP." Click Next. Select "Add a custom connection (for example TCP/IP)." Click Next. Now, when you go back to the Signon screen you should be able to choose from calling AOL via an AOL phone number or an "ISP/LAN Connection." You make the selection in the drop-down box under "Select Location." Now, connect to your Internet service as you normally would, then fire up AOL's software and from the Signon screen select "ISP/LAN Connection."

Having Problems with
Your America Online Connection?
Head to the Members Helping Members forum on America Online for the best tech support on the service. Type the key-words **members helping members** in the location bar at the top of the screen to get there. This will take you to a public dis-cussion area where you're sure to find other members who are having the same problem as you are—or who know the solution.

◆ CABLE TV OFFERS HIGH SPEED INTERNET, BUT AT A PRICE

Many local cable TV franchises offer Internet access through the same cable that sends you cable TV. With advertised connect rates of 10 megabytes per second, it's no wonder cable Internet is getting popular—although actual connect rates can be con-siderably lower depending upon what time of day you tap in. Cable Internet costs about $150 for installation, plus $40 to $50 per month. (That may be a good deal if you're getting gouged by local phone rates to call AOL or an ISP.) Cable Internet is presently available in limited areas, though access is sure to grow. To find out if you can get it, call your local cable TV franchise. When you call for prices ask how many outlets are included in the installation fee (cable TVs and cable modems can't connect to the same outlet), and make sure you can actually connect to the Internet before your cable installer leaves. (Gloria uses a combination of America Online and cable access. If you decide to go this route sign up for AOL's "Bring Your Own Access" subscription option for the cheapest rate.)

◆ SATELLITE IS PRICEY, BUT THE ONLY OPTION IN SOME RURAL AREAS

If phone calls to the nearest ISP are eating into your budget and cable Internet isn't available in your area—or if you're like some stitchers we know who've retired to life on a boat—consider accessing the Internet via satellite. The main requirements are a Windows 95 or NT-running PC, a direct line of sight to the southern horizon, and a lot of patience. Hughes Network System's **DirecPC** (**http://www.direcpc.com**) is the leading satellite Internet service. Cost runs about $300 for the antenna and software, plus a $50 startup fee and $50 per month. You'll probably need to spend another $200-$300 to get the antenna installed properly on your roof (aiming it is much harder than aiming a TV satellite dish).

You'll also need to sign up for an ISP. You'll probably want a national one, and also one that has actually been tested with satellite transmission. You also want an ISP that permits subscribers to access their mail and newsgroups by an account other than one on their system. You can access AOL through a satellite link, but you'll need to use an ISP as an intermediary.

Many people love DirecPC, others hate it (tech support is lousy). If you sign up, tap into the Usenet newsgroup **alt.satellite.direcpc** for support.

❓ WHAT ABOUT "FREE E-MAIL" SERVICES?

There are two types of free e-mail services. One is **Juno** (**http://www.juno.com**), which gives you free software that you use to dial local access numbers and send and retrieve mail. The other option is Web-based services like Microsoft's **Hotmail** (**http://www.hotmail.com**). You tap into these Web services through a computer that already has some Internet access—a work computer for instance, or one at a library or cyber-cafe.

Their advantage is that you can send and retrieve private e-mail through the service without using, for instance, your work e-mail address if you're tapping in through your work computer.

Juno is a great deal, especially if there's a local access number in your area. In fact, many branches of the military recommend it as an economical way for military families to e-mail loved ones stationed abroad. But all you get is e-mail, unless you put up $20/month for Web access.

There are some big disadvantages to using "free e-mail" services like Juno and Hotmail. Most notably, you may not be able to participate in some of the high-volume needlework discussion mailing lists. These lists generate lots of e-mail each day—so much mail that it will quickly fill up your mailbox on these services and the mailing list will unsubscribe you. In fact, some mailing lists won't even permit people to subscribe who are using free e-mail services like Hotmail or Yahoo. It's best to get a "real" e-mail account with an ISP or online service like America Online, Compuserve, or Microsoft Network.

T
I
P

Be Security Conscious

When your computer is connected to the Net via cable it's basically a node in the wide-area network of your neighborhood. Because certain cable modems forward the NetBios protocol onto that network, users of certain cable Internet services occasionally have found they have access to their neighbors' hard drives. The cable service can deploy various security techniques to prevent that, but you need to take precautions too. Turn off Windows 95/98's printer and file sharing by clicking Start/Settings/Control Panel. Double-click the Network icon. Click the File and Print Sharing button. Uncheck the boxes "I want to be able to give others access to my files" and "I want to be able to allow others to print to my printer(s)." Click OK. If you're running Windows 95 you should also download from the **Microsoft** Web site (**http://www.microsoft.com**) and install the Windows 95 Service Pack, which includes security fixes. If you're using a Mac head to the Control Panel and select File Sharing. Make sure it's Off.

ANATOMY OF A WEB BROWSER

Whether you tap into the Web through an Internet service, America Online, or a cable or satellite connection, the software centerpiece of your Web surfing will be what's called a browser. In the old days you needed different sorts of software to do different things on the Net. For instance, you needed mail software to send and receive e-mail, a newsreader to read public discussions, and special software called FTP for "file download protocol" to download files to your computer. Plus you needed a browser to view (or browse through) the graphical portion of the Internet known as the Web. Now all these functions are built into browsers.

Most computers are sold with Netscape's Navigator or Microsoft's Internet Explorer already installed. You can also download them for free from **Netscape's** Web site (**http://www.netscape.com**) or from **Microsoft's** (**http://www.microsoft.com**).

While you can use just about any computer to log onto the Internet in some fashion (even an original Apple II circa 1979), to be able to view graphics you'll need a computer manufactured in at least the last 8 years. If you have an older computer download a copy of the $35 **Opera Browser** (**http://www.operasoftware.com**) which will run on any Windows 3.x-running PCs as old as a 386SX with at least 6 megabytes of RAM.

If you're running an older Macintosh, head to Chris Adams' **Web Browsers for Antique Macs** web page (**http://www.edprint.demon.co.uk/se/macweb.html**) and download Tradewave's MacWeb or an early version of NCSA Mosaic.

If you've never configured Internet software before, you'll need someone to help you, even if you're a computer genius (believe us, we know). Your ISP will (or should) give you directions on how to set up Windows 95 or the Macintosh OS to at least log on to their service.

But once you're connected, you're pretty much on your own. That's why we've put together this little tutorial.

Use a Different Web Browser with America Online

Internet Explorer comes with some versions of America Online's software, but you can use Netscape's Navigator instead if you prefer (and many people do). Here's how: dial up AOL and make the connection. Minimize America Online's software. Fire up Navigator. Type the Web address you want to head to and you're there.

Keep Your Browser Current to Keep Your Computer Secure

Hardly a month goes by without someone finding a new security hole in a popular browser—and its maker quickly plugging it. Keep your Web browser current—and your e-mail software too, by visiting the Web sites of their makers regularly and downloading any security patches or new versions. Be sure you download those only from their makers' Web sites. There have been reports of people receiving via e-mail "security patches" for Microsoft products that were actually hacker code to steal passwords. You can find out what version of Netscape you have by pulling down the Help menu and selecting About Communicator. If it's less than 4.5 you need to download a new version from **Netscape** Web site (**http://www.netscape.com**). If you're running Internet Explorer, select About Internet Explorer from the Help menu. If you're running a version prior to 5.0, you need to download a new copy from the **Microsoft** Web site (**http://www.microsoft.com**).

The following directions are for the latest versions of Explorer and Navigator, but, with the exception of the instructions for e-mail, most will work with earlier versions of the browsers.

◆ HOW TO TAP INTO A WEB PAGE

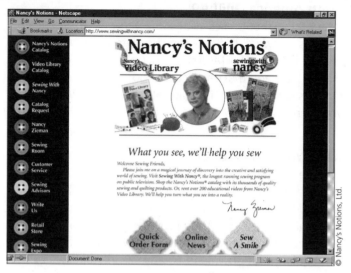

To get to a Web page, type its address, also known as its URL, or Universal Resource Locator, into the Address: bar in Navigator, or the Location: bar in Internet Explorer. (In older Web browsers you must preface the address with http: as in **http://www.sewingwithnancy.com**, but in new browsers you can type simply **www.sewingwithnancy.com** or even **sewingwithnancy.com**).

Take note that the case of the letters is important.

You can also cut and paste URLs from other documents into the address or location bar. (Highlight the address with your mouse, press Ctrl-C, or Command-C on a Mac, then place the mouse in the location bar and press Ctrl-V, or Command-V on a Mac, to paste it in. Then hit **<Enter>**.)

To move to other pages in the Web site, click on highlighted words, or, whenever you move your cursor over an object and it changes into a hand, right-click to follow the link.

What does all that gobbledygook in a URL mean?
The http: tells your Internet service what kind of document
you are trying to access on the Internet. **Http** stands for
"hyper-text transfer protocol," the protocol of the Web.
You might run into **ftp**: which stands for "file transfer protocol," an early Internet scheme for transferring files. The
protocol is always followed by // which separates it from
the document's address.

Next comes the domain name—for example,
www.ctpub.com. The triple-w designates C&T's Web subdi-
rectory on its Internet server. The .com suffix indicates that
C&T is a commercial entity. If C&T were a university it
would have an .edu suffix, or .org if it were a non-profit.
The words that follow the domain name, separated by
slashes, designate further subdirectories. Many, though not
all, URLs end with a specific file name.

◆ FIND YOUR WAY AROUND THE WEB WITHOUT GETTING LOST

- Click the Back button in your browser to return to previously
  visited Web sites.
- Click the History button or select the history feature from a
  drop-down menu to list previously visited URLs.
- Or click your browser's drop-down location box, which displays the last dozen or so URLs that you have actually typed
  into the browser (in other words, it doesn't display links that
  you've clicked on something to get to).

How to Find the Web Site if the Web Page Isn't There

URLs point you to directories on a remote computer just like directory paths (c:\windows\programs) get you to different directories and subdirectories on your computer's hard disk.

If a Web address doesn't get you to what you want, try working back through the URL. For example, sewing-machine maker Elna offers a pattern for a "Pet Placemat" on their Web site at:

http://www.elnausa.com/projects/99feb/99feb.htm

But if it's not there when you get there, try:
http://www.elnausa.com/projects/99feb

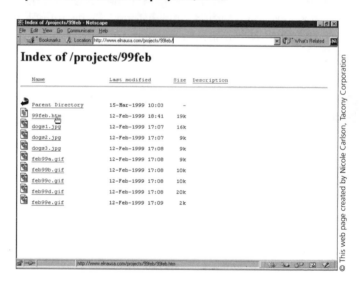

© This web page created by Nicole Carlson, Tacony Corporation

This might get you to a directory that lists files which you can click on to attempt to view or download. (Hint: If you see a file with an htm or html at the end of its name, click on it. That's a Web page document.) But if this URL doesn't get you anything, or you get an error message like "Access denied," try going further back through the URL to: **http://www.elnausa.com/projects**

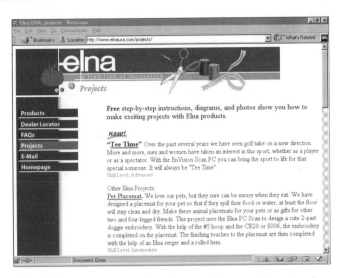

Ah, this displays a directory! But say, for argument's sake, that this URL doesn't display anything worthwhile, or you get another error message. Try Elna's home page at the URL root at: **http://www.elnausa.com**

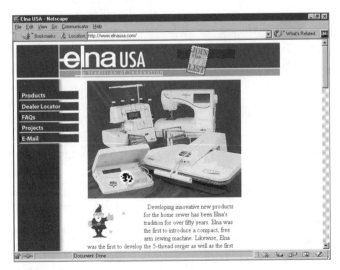

Here's Elna's home page, at the "root" of the URL.

HOW TO USE BOOKMARKS

Web browsers let you "bookmark" sites so that you can visit them again simply by fishing through your bookmark catalog. You usually just click a bookmark icon (or Favorites in Internet Explorer) or select the feature from a toolbar to add the Web site you're currently visiting to your bookmark list.

COMMON ERROR MESSAGES
WHEN YOU ENTER A WEB ADDRESS

✋ **404 Not Found**
The requested URL/blocks/tips.html was not found on this server.

Reason: Your browser was able to find the Internet service or the computer on which the Web site was or is hosted, but no such page was found on the service. (The very last word "word" at the end of a URL is the page's address. For example, "tips.html.") Maybe the Web site owner removed that particular page. Or perhaps the Web site no longer exists.

Fix: Try working back through the URL as explained in the above tip, to see if you can locate the Web site, or determine if the site itself is gone from the service. Also, try suffixing the page's address with "htm" or "html" instead of its current extension. For example, in place of **tips.html** type **tips.htm**. (An HTML suffix is the same as HTM, but some Web page hosting services require that Web pages be named with one or the other. Typing the wrong extension is a common mistake.)

✋ **DNS Lookup Failure** *or*
Unable to locate the server. The server does not have a DNS entry.

Reason: DNS stands for "domain name server." A domain name is the first part of a URL—for example, in **www.ctpub.com**, ctpub.com is the domain name. Every Internet service (and AOL) has a database of such Web page host Links addresses. When

**You Can Add Shortcuts to
Web Sites on Your Windows Desktop.**
Say there's a particular Web site you like to visit everyday. If
you're running Windows 95/98 you can add a shortcut to it
from your desktop. When you click on the shortcut your browser will load, dial your Internet service, and speed you to the
Web site. Use your mouse to drag the site's URL, either from a

you type a URL, the first thing your browser does is tell your
Internet service to look up the domain name in its database, to
find out where it's located. If it can't find it, your Internet service's computer may poll other domain name directories around
the Internet to determine if any of them know where the
domain name can be found. If none of them do, you may get
the error message "DNS Lookup Failure."

Why can't they find the domain name? Maybe it no
longer exists. Or perhaps it's so new that the domain name
databases your Internet service uses can't find it. Sometimes
you also get this error message when there's heavy traffic
on the Internet. Your Internet service is taking too long to
look up the name, so your browser errors out.

Fix: Try typing the URL into your browser later in the
day. If you still get the error message, try the URL a few
days later, or even a week. If you still get error messages
the domain name no longer exists.

 No Response from Server

Reason: Your browser is unable to get a timely
response from the Web site's host computer. This can hap-
pen during heavy traffic on the Internet or on the branch
of the Internet you are traveling. It can be because the computer that's hosting the Web site is overloaded (everyone is
tapping in). Or it can be because your Internet service is
overloaded, or its own computers are experiencing slow-
downs for technical reasons.

Fix: Try the URL again, either in a few minutes or later
in the day.

link in a Web page, or, if you're using Internet Explorer, drag from the Address bar to the Favorites menu or to the left of the Links bar. If you're using Netscape, drag the icon to the left of Location: when a page is loaded. Your mouse cursor should change into a circle with a slash as you drag the URL to the desktop.

You Can Customize Your Browser's Personal Toolbar by Adding Bookmarks.

You can customize the personal toolbar in Communicator or the Links bar in Internet Explorer by adding not only icons for frequently visited URLs, but also folders of bookmarks. In Communicator add a URL to the personal toolbar by dragging a link from a Web page or by dragging the icon to the left of Location: when a page is loaded. To add a folder instead, click the Bookmarks icon, select Edit Bookmarks, and highlight the folder you wish to place on the toolbar. Right-click and select Set as Toolbar Folder. In Internet Explorer you can similarly customize the Links bar by adding individual URLs as well as folders. Drag folders from the Favorites menu to add them to the Links bar. To add a URL to the link bar drag it from the Address bar to the left of the Links bar, from the Favorites menu, or from a Web page.

You Can Use Third-Party Bookmark Software to Organize Your Bookmarks.

There are a lot of low-cost utilities for organizing bookmarks that you can download from the Web. These are particularly handy if you're using two browsers—both Netscape and Internet Explorer for example. They enable you to store your bookmarks in a central location, and organize them into folders with icons—in a more efficient manner than your browser will allow. Some utilities also let you password-protect bookmarks. A good spot to download them is C/net's **Shareware.Com** (**http://www.shareware.com**). Search for the phrase "bookmark organizer." One we like for PCs is the free program LinkMan from Thomas Reimann. For Macs we like URL Manager Pro, the $25 shareware program from **Alco Blom** (**http://www.url-manager.com**).

◆ HOW TO PRINT WEB PAGES, OR SELECTIONS FROM PAGES

You can print entire Web pages just like you'd print any other
document on your computer screen.

First, wait until the page is transmitted to your computer in its
entirety. In Navigator you'll see what looks like snow falling
through the big "N" logo in the top right-hand corner of the
screen. If you're using a Mac you'll see shooting stars. That means
the page is being transmitted to your computer. In Explorer, the
"e" logo in the top right-hand corner spins as the page is downloading. When the logo animation stops, your page is complete.

To print in Navigator, pull down the File menu and select
Print Preview. Once you click the Print button in the Preview
window, you'll get a dialog box from which you can choose
which pages of the currently viewed Web page you wish to
print. On a Macintosh, pull down the File menu and select Print.

In Internet Explorer, pull down the File menu and select Print.

On more complex Web sites your browser might ask you to
specify which frame you'd like to print. A frame is a division of
the page (a page with multiple frames is usually framed by multiple scroll bars). You will need to go back to the page and
mouse-click the side or section you wish to print, then head
back to the printing menu to print it.

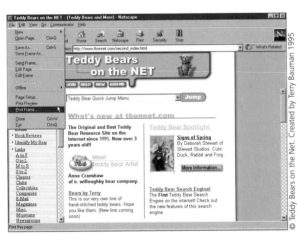

*Teddy Bears on
the Net, a Web
site for Teddy
makers and
lovers, has
frames–divisions
that you can
click between
and scroll
through individ-
ually. In order to
print material*

*on a framed page you must first click on the side of the page you wish to print in
order to select it, then select Print or Print Preview from your browser's File menu.*

You can also print sections of a Web page by highlighting with your mouse the sections you wish to print, copying them into the clipboard, then pasting the clipboard contents into your word processor and printing from there.

Remember, Web Pages Are Copyrighted! Web pages are copyrighted just as any publication is, or any needlework design, for that matter. You should not print them except for your own personal use without asking permission from the Web page's owner. The same holds true for any elements on the page, including both text and graphics. Never, ever print or distribute these things—or, heaven forbid, put them on your own Web page.

HOW TO SAVE WEB PAGES TO YOUR COMPUTER'S DISK

You can save entire Web pages to your disk so that you can peruse them later, but keep in mind the above warning—these pages are copyrighted and you should not distribute them.

First the page must be completely loaded.

Remember to click on the frame you wish to save.

In your browser, from the File menu select Save as... A pop-up box will give you a choice of saving the page as HTML or text. If you're using a Mac, the pop-up box will give you the option of saving the text as source, which is the same as HTML.

HTML is the coding that is used to format Web pages—it's similar to text, but with a few weird notations thrown in. Save the page in HTML format if you plan to view it with your browser later, while you're off-line. (To view it in your browser later, select Open Page from the File menu. On a Mac, select Open Page in Navigator. Click Choose File, then click your way to the file stored on your hard disk. Once you've found it, click the Open button.)

If you want to merely pull up the Web page's text in your word processor, and perhaps print it later, save it as text.

Neither of these features will let you save the page's images, however. You'll need to save each graphic individually.

◆ HOW TO CAPTURE IMAGES
◆ YOU FIND ON THE INTERNET

Images on Web pages are copyrighted just like text is. If you want to use them in any way—either to print to distribute to your friends or post on your own Web pages—the same rules apply as to text: you need to ask the owner's permission first!

Position your cursor over the image and right-click. On a Mac, click-hold. A menu box will pop up. Select Save Image As... or Save Picture As....You can later view it in either your browser or a graphics program like Paint Shop Pro. You can even import it into a word processing document. (In Microsoft Word, select Picture from the Insert menu.)

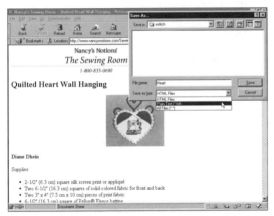

Your browser will let you save Web pages either as plain text or with their HTML formatting, but neither option will save graphics. You'll need to save each image individually.

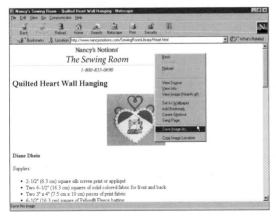

In order to save a picture off the Web, right click on it in Windows or click-hold on a Mac and select Save as... Remember, though, that these images are copyrighted by their artists and you should not print or distribute them without asking permission first.

◆ HOW TO DOWNLOAD SOFTWARE FROM THE INTERNET

In most instances all you need to do is click on the highlighted name of the program or file on a Web page and your browser will start downloading—hopefully by prompting you where you want to store the file.

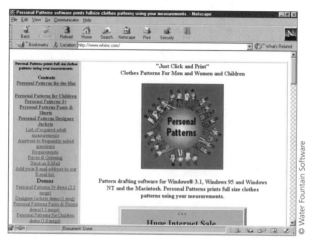

*From the Web site of **Water Fountain Software** (**www.wfsinc.com**), you can download demos of the sewing software Personal Patterns, which you can use to generate custom garment patterns.*

Once you click on the file name your browser will ask you where on your com-puter you want to store the software. Once you select a directory, click Save.

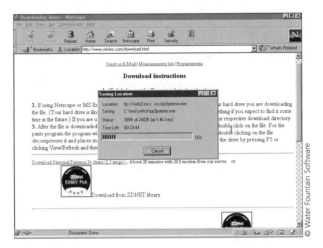

© Water Fountain Software

Once the file begins transferring, this box will pop up, showing you the progress of the download.

If the file transfer progress box disappears, don't panic. Its disappearance doesn't mean your computer has stopped downloading the file. For instance, it may disappear if you click on something else on the Web page or in your browser. You will probably find the transfer box tucked away in some other corner of your computer screen (like the bottom program status bar) and the transfer still faithfully chugging away in the background.

TIP

Say you can't get your browser to download software in a sane fashion. Maybe it spits kooky characters across the screen when you try, or has some other unhelpful response. There's a simple way out: right-click on the file name in Windows or click-hold on a Mac so this menu box pops up. Select Save Link As... and you'll be on your way.

One thing to keep in mind is that if the file transfer progress box flashes on your screen, then disappears, your browser may not have saved the file. That will be because it's not tapped into the correct Web page to actually download the file. You should be on the Web page that displays the highlighted file name, or a "Download now" link. In other words, you need to be only one mouse click away from the file download in order to get this to work.

❓ What Do You Do With Software After You Download It, or What Does that ZIP or SIT at the End of Its Name Mean?

When you download software from a Web site it's usually compressed. That means that the file has been shrunk so that it takes less time to transfer to your computer.

PKZIP by **PKWare** (**http://www.pkware.com**) is the most commonly used compression format in the PC world. When a file has a .ZIP extension it has been compressed with PKZIP. You'll need to download PKZIP in order to uncompress it. A handy (in fact indispensable) utility to have is the $29 shareware program **WinZip** by Nico Mak (**http://www.winzip.com**). It will de-ZIP those files for you automatically.

Stuffit, a free program by **Aladdin Software** (**http://www.aladdinsys.com**) is the compression program used with Macintoshes. Software compressed with Stuffit ends with .SIT, and you'll need to download Stuffit in order to expand it.

What about files ending with .EXE? They're self-extracting, which means that you merely click on them in order to uncompress them.

As a file download starts, always check that the file is writing itself to your disk with the same name as it had on the remote computer, so you know what to do with it.

◆ HOW TO SEND E-MAIL

If you're using America Online, all you need to do is click on the You Have Mail icon on the greeting screen to read your e-mail or send mail, even out on the Internet. (To send messages to someone on the Internet from AOL type the full Internet address—for example **ctinfo@ctpub.com**—into the To: line in the AOL mail screen just as you'd type an AOL address.)

If you're using an Internet service you can use special mail software like Eudora or Pegasus. Or you can use the mail program built into your browser.

In Navigator, press Ctrl-2 to get to the mail box. On a Mac, click the Mail icon box in the lower right-hand corner of the browser's screen to get to your in-box. Command-T retrieves new e-mail.

In Explorer, click the Mail icon in the upper right-hand corner of the browser's screen to load the Outlook Express mail program.

Unfortunately, You Will Need to Set Up Your Browser's Mail Program to Be Able to Send Mail

In order for your browser to send and retrieve mail through your ISP for the first time, you'll need to tell it the name of your ISP's computer where it stores mail.

If you're in a pinch, and for some reason you don't know the name of this computer, you might be able to guess: it's probably "mail.*yourdomain*.com." Regardless, your Internet service should tell you the name of the computer where it stores mail so you can enter this vital information into your mail program. That, your Internet e-mail address, and your password are essentially all the browser needs to know to be able to send and receive mail.

 Setting Up Mail in Navigator

You can set up Navigator to send and retrieve mail through your ISP by heading to this setup box. Get to it by selecting Preferences from the Edit menu, then scrolling through the setup menu list on the left. Under the Mail & Groups category, select Mail Server. Type in the user name you 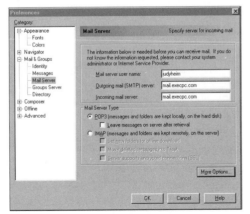 *use with your ISP and the names of the incoming and outgoing mail servers. Click OK when you're finished.*

◆ Setting Up Mail in Explorer

In Explorer's Outlook Express, select Accounts from the Tools menu. Click the Add button and select Mail to start the wizard that will guide you through the mail set-up process.

When Outlook Express is set up success-fully to send and retrieve mail you should have a settings box similar to this (you can reach it by pulling down the Tools menu and selecting Accounts. Head to the Mail tab, highlight the account name, and click the Properties button). Judy's e-mail address is judyheim@execpc.com, so notice that her outgoing SMTP mail serv-er is named mail.execpc.com. Even if your ISP gave you erroneous directions for set-

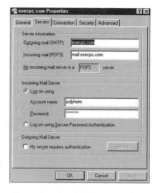

ting up your mail program, you can make a few simple deductions from your e-mail address to fill in the blanks.

◆ Sending and Receiving Mail with Navigator

Press Ctrl-2 to get to Navigator's mail program. On a Mac, click the Mail icon box in the lower right-hand corner of the brows-er's screen. To download your mail from your Internet service, click the Get Msg icon, then type your ISP password when prompted.

To send a message, click the New Msg icon. After you're fin-ished writing, click the Send icon to dial your ISP and send it immediately. Or pull down the File menu and select Send Later for Navigator to store it in the outbox.

You can write your message in different fonts and colors with Navigator's mail pro-gram. You can even add pictures by heading to the Insert menu and selecting Image. But

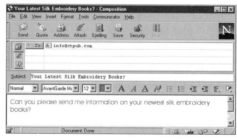

your recipient won't be able to see the special effects unless they're using another HTML-compatible mail program like that in Explorer.

Sending and Receiving Mail with Explorer

Head to Outlook Express by clicking the Mail icon in Explorer's right-hand corner. Press Ctrl-N, or Command-N on a Mac, to pop up a message composition form. When you're done writing, click the Send button. Take note that this will only store the message in Outlook's outbox. To actually send it you need to click the Send and Receive button on the top of Outlook's main screen so that the program dials your Internet service and checks and sends mail.

T I P

Can you (or should you) send e-mail messages festooned with pictures and color?

The mail programs found in the latest versions of Explorer and Navigator are what's called HTML or rich text compatible. That means you can use them to send and read mail with the same kind of formatting found on Web pages. And the same sorts of pictures too, like GIF and JPG images. America Online can also send and read *some* HTML coding in messages, but not all.

Should you bedeck your e-mail with pictures of pictures of yourself and your sewing projects? Probably not.

First, graphics take *much* longer than text to download. And no one likes to sit twiddling their fingers as their mail program chugs to capture some humongous e-mail message they were not expecting.

Second, many people use text-only e-mail programs like Eudora that will display that rich text as gibberish.

Maybe this will change someday. Maybe everyone will have super-fast links into the Internet and HTML-friendly e-mail programs. Until then, write your messages in old-fashioned plain text. (That means avoiding Explorer's "stationery" feature, and turning off the rich text setting. You can find it by pulling down the Tools menu and selecting Options. Under the Send tab, check Plain Text, then click the Apply button.)

◆ HOW TO TALK TO OTHER STITCHERS ON THE INTERNET

There are several ways besides e-mail that let you talk to stitchers around the world.

⌐ Message Boards on Web Sites

Many stitching Web sites offer message or bulletin boards where you can post and read messages on topics ranging from batting brands to piecing techniques. Often these discussions are lively and informative, because they're so easy to tap into and they remain on the Web site for so long. All you need to join in is to type the URL into your browser.

⌐ Usenet Newsgroups

Newsgroups are public messages you post over the Internet in bulletin board style. There are seven specifically devoted to textiles:

alt.fashion
alt.sewing
rec.crafts.textiles.misc
rec.crafts.textiles.marketplace
rec.crafts.textiles.needlework
rec.crafts.textiles.quilting
rec.crafts.textiles.sewing

As you can see they are named like subdirectories on a computer. To tap in you'd use the news feature of your browser, or special news reading software.

⌐ Mailing Lists

You'll find dozens of mailing lists devoted to different stitching topics. Mailing lists are also where you find the most worthwhile information on the Internet on just about any topic.

You don't tap into a Web site to participate. Instead, you send an e-mail message to a computer (or person) to subscribe to the list. Each day, e-mail from other members of the mailing list finds its way to your mailbox. To participate in the discussion you send your message to a central computer that broadcasts it to everyone on the list.

▶ Online Service Discussion Forums

All the major online services, including America Online, Compuserve, and Microsoft Network, offer lively stitching discussion forums.

▶ Chat Rooms

Aren't chat rooms those notorious dens where lascivious strangers type to each other at 2 a.m.? Yes, but stitchers also enjoy getting together to chat, both on the Internet and on online services like America Online. Some sewing Web sites also offer chat areas for visitors.

You can chat with other stitchers on America Online in the Crafts Community chat room. To get there, use the keyword sewing. Click the Crafts Chat Room to get to the chat room.

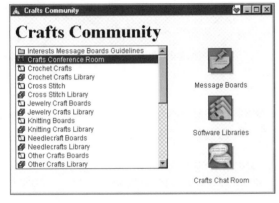

*About.Com's sewing forum (**http://sewing.about.com**) hosts online chats every evening. To participate you need only to be running version 3.x or higher of Netscape or Internet Explorer,*

and you must have Java enabled. Other sewing sites also offer chat rooms. To participate you may need to download special software. You'll need to read the directions on the Web site to find out how to join in.

What's ICQ?

ICQ, named after the Internet acronym "I Seek You," is a free chat program similar to America Online's Instant Messenger. Once you install it, whenever you tap into the Internet, it "logs" you into the ICQ network, informing your friends that you've come online. And it tells you if they're online. You can send each other instant messages, exchange files, and chat as if you were both in an Internet chat room. It offers a number of privacy features that go beyond those in AOL's Instant Messenger. You can set ICQ to tell friends that you're online, but don't wish to be disturbed, for instance. You can also set ICQ to prevent strangers from sending you unsolicited messages. You can download ICQ in both PC and Mac flavors from **Mirabilis** (**http://www.mirabilis.com**).

◆ HOW TO READ USENET NEWSGROUPS WITH YOUR WEB BROWSER

Participating in Web site message boards or mailing lists is fairly straightforward, so long as you know how to use your Web browser and mail program. But setting up your browser to read newsgroups can be tricky. The first time you want to read a newsgroup you'll need to download a list of current newsgroups from your Internet service. Then you'll need to search it and subscribe to the groups you're interested in. Finally, you need to download the messages themselves. Here's how to do it with Navigator and Explorer:

How to Read the Usenet Stitching Newsgroups with Navigator

1. You must first set up your browser to retrieve newsgroups from your Internet server. Find out from your Internet server the name of the computer where new groups are stored. (It will be something like groups.myisp.com.) Pull down the Edit menu and select Preferences. Under Mail & Groups, head to the Group Server setup box and enter your ISP information. Click OK to save it.

First, tell Navigator the name of the server on your ISP where newsgroups are stored.

2. Connect to your Internet service.

3. Head to Navigator's message center by pressing Ctrl-2, or click the Mail icon box in the lower-right hand corner of the browser's screen on a Mac.

4. From the File menu, select Subscribe to Discussion Groups.

5. Click the All Groups tab to download a list of current newsgroups. This may take a while since the list is large. The message "Receiving discussion groups" should appear on the very bottom line of the screen.

Download the complete list of newsgroups in order to search for the ones on needlework.

6. When that humongous list of newsgroups has finished downloading, head to the Search for a Group tab. Type "crafts" (or whatever you're interested in) in the search box and click the Search Now button. Type "textiles" instead to get a full list of all the needlecraft-related newsgroups.

7. Once the newsgroup searcher has come up with a list of inter-esting newsgroups, highlight the one you want to read, and press the Subscribe button. A check will appear beside it.

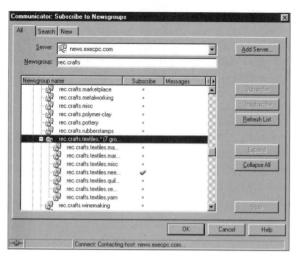

After you download and search the newsgroups, subscribe to the groups you want to read by selecting them. You can click through the list just as you'd click through subdirectories on your computer.

8. To read your newsgroup, head back to the message center (Ctrl-2, or click the Mail icon box on a Mac). From the pull-down menu box at the top of the screen, select the newsgroup and click Download Messages. You may want to download only a selection (under 500 for example) and mark the rest of the messages as read. This way, the next time you download messages from the newsgroup, you will only download the newest ones.

9. From the Go menu you can move from thread to thread, read-ing some messages and skipping others.

10. To read messages in the future, go to the message center (Ctrl-2, or click the Mail icon box on a Mac). From the pull-down menu box at the top of the screen, select the newsgroup you want to read. From the File menu select Get Messages/New.

Select the messages and message threads you want to read and they'll appear at the bottom of the screen. (If you don't get a split screen you

may need to "pull up" the bottom portion of the screen with your mouse. In other words, the window is there; it's just hidden.)

 ## How to Read the Usenet Stitching Newsgroups with Explorer

1. Load the Outlook Express mail portion of Internet Explorer by clicking on the mailbox icon on the top right-hand corner of the screen. Click

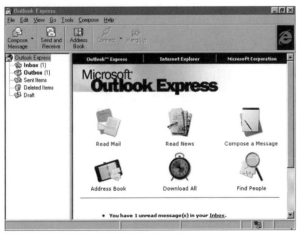

the Read News icon on the Express screen. If you have not yet set it up to read newsgroups with your ISP, a setup wizard will appear. It will prompt you for your name, e-mail address, and the name of the dial-up connection you use to connect to your ISP. Most important of all, it will ask you the name of the server on your ISP where the news messages can be found.

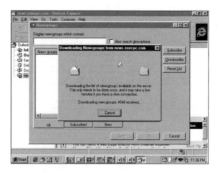

2. *The next time you click the Read News icon it will ask you if you'd like to download a list of the newsgroups from your ISP. This may take a while since there are tens of thousands of newsgroups.*

3. *Type "textiles" to search the list for newsgroups that contain "textiles" in their name, and to get a full list of the needlework-related newsgroups. Subscribe to them by highlighting each one and clicking the Subscribe button. Then click OK when you're done.*

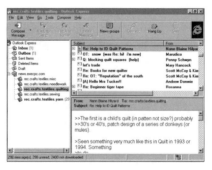

4. *To read the newsgroups you've subscribed to, click on the name of each newsgroup on the left side of the screen. To read individual messages, click on the headers displayed at the top right of the screen.*

How to Read the Usenet
Stitching Newsgroups on America Online

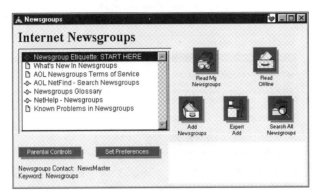

1. *To read the Internet newsgroups through AOL press Ctrl-k, or Command-k on a Mac, and type the keyword newsgroups. Click on the Search All Newsgroups icon to search the tens of thousands of newsgroups for ones in your interests. (Some useful search words are: quilting, textiles, cross-stitch, sewing, knitting, and weaving.)*

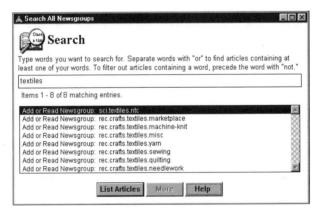

2. *Once you click the Search Newsgroups icon, type your search word and press Search. Once AOL comes up with a list of matching newsgroups, click the Add button to add selected newsgroups to the list of newsgroups that you wish to read, or click on the name of the newsgroup and from the pop-up box click on "Subscribe to newsgroup."*

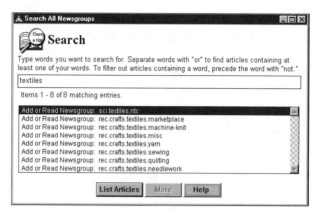

3. Depending on which version of AOL's software you're using you may be able read the messages in the newly subscribed newsgroup immediately. Otherwise you'll need to head back to the main newsgroup menu by closing the windows (click the X in the upper right-hand corner). Click the Read My Newsgroups button to pop up a list of the newsgroups to which you're subscribed. Click the List Unread button to list messages in the newsgroups you haven't read yet.

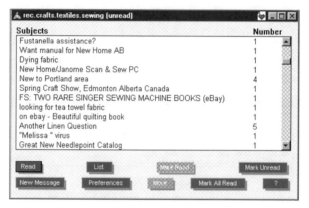

4. To read listed messages and their replies, highlight each message and click the Read button.

**Read Usenet Textile
Newsgroups from Your Browser**
You can read the textile newsgroups from the comfort of your
Web browser by heading to **Dejanews**
(**http://www.dejanews.com**). Reading them through this Web
site isn't as easy as reading them with your browser's newsreader, but it's a simple way to access the groups.

◆ HOW TO FIND PATTERNS,
PEOPLE, PRODUCTS, AND MORE!

Looking for help with your Pfaff? How about a friend you
shared a sewing machine with in high school? To quickly find
what—or who—you're looking for on the Internet all you need
to do is head to one of these big searchers:

EXCITE
http://www.excite.com

DOGPILE
http://www.dogpile.com

WHOWHERE? PEOPLE FINDER
http://www.whowhere.lycos.com

Type the name of the pattern or person you're looking for—or
even the name of a recipe or rare disease—and the searcher will
come up with a list of possibly applicable Web sites or directory
hits. Usually you can find at least one information-filled Web site
within the first two "pages" of matches. From that page you
can scuttle around the Web, to related links and Web pages.

CHAPTER 2

sewers' Favorite Web Hang-Outs

S ometimes when you're sewing it's nice to take a break—get a cookie, saunter to the computer and check your e-mail. These Web sites are great spots to take a "computer break" when the frustrations of pressing a cuff or hemming stretch knit overwhelm you. You'll read tips, articles on topics ranging from interfacing to sewing chiffon, plus recommendations on where to buy hard-to-find fabric and notions. Many of these sites also offer bulletin boards or chat features so you can correspond with other sewers.

Throughout the book we've used a "sewing bee" icon to mark those Web sites that offer bulletin board or chat features so sewers can converse.

HOME SEWING ASSOCIATION
http://www.sewing.org

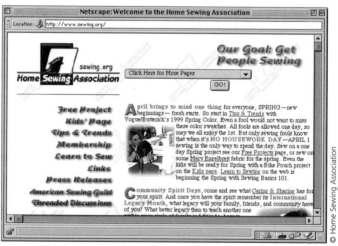

You'll find directions for sewing projects, a kids page, and lots of tips on topics such as how to take measurements. In the HSA's very active bulletin board area you'll find other sewers solving one another's problems.

DELPHI'S NEEDLE & THREAD FORUM
http://www0.delphi.com/needle

*Judy Smith's forum offers an active message board and chat fea-
ture for sewers, a directory of Internet resources for sewers, and
much more.*

COMPUSERVE'S SEWING & QUILTING FORUM
http://forumsb.compuserve.com/gvforums/default.asp?srv=sewing

If you're a subscriber to the online service Compuserve use the
go word **sewing** to get to its wonderful sewing forum. If
you're not, head to the above URL with your Web browser
where you can still access its well-populated message forum for
sewers and a terrific file library where you can download patterns, directions, and all sorts of goodies.

SANDRA BETZINA ONLINE
http://www.sandrabetzina.com

*Read columns and tips from sewing guru Sandra Betzina. You'll
find lots of good stuff on her site, including a bulletin board for
sewers and links to other Web resources for sewers.*

NANCY'S NOTIONS ONLINE
http://www.nancysnotions.com

*Click the Sewing Room icon to read free articles or download free
project sheets. There's also a very active message board for sewers.*

SEWING AT ABOUT.COM
http://sewing.about.com

*Debbie Colgrove is your host at this marvelous sewing resource
where you'll find how-tos, articles, tips, and links to all the best
sewing resources on the Net.*

SEW SOMETHING EXCITING
http://pages.prodigy.net/shereemckee/sewsomething.htm

Sheree McKee offers sewing tips, thread advice, serger sugges-tions, shareware machine embroidery designs, and lots of links to other Internet resources for sewers.

Surf the Ring of Stitchers
Visit the Web pages of other sewers by surfing Elaine Rieck's **Machine Embroidery and Sewing Enthusiasts Ring (http://members.home.net/erieck/form.htm)**. You don't have to "join" the ring in order to surf it. Merely click "Next" in the ring's logo to surf to the next site.

Web Sites for Sewing TV Shows

Many of these sites offer tips and an occasional free pattern, in addition to information about specific shows. If you're a die-hard fan of sewing TV shows, stop in at **Telecrafter (http://www.banamba.com/telecrafter)** which offers a mailing list discussion for fans of these shows.

ALEENE'S CREATIVE LIVING
http://www.aleenes.com/television/index.html

THE CAROL DUVALL SHOW
http://www.hgtv.com/shows/CDS.shtml

MARTHA PULLEN'S SEWING ROOM
http://www.cptr.ua.edu/msr.htm

QUILTING AND SEWING WITH KAYE WOOD
http://www.kayewood.com/index.html

SEW CREATIVE WITH DONNA WILDER
http://www.poly-fil.com/sewcreative/SC.html

SEW PERFECT WITH SANDRA BETZINA
http://www.hgtv.com/shows/SEW.shtml

SEWING CONNECTION WITH SHIRLEY ADAMS
http://www.sewingconnection.com

SEWING TODAY
http://linex1.linex.com/jandk/sewing.html

SEWING WITH NANCY ZIEMAN
http://www.nancysnotions.com/SWN.html

SIMPLY QUILTS
http://www.hgtv.com/shows/QLT.shtml

 Web Sites for Sewing Magazines

You can sometimes find articles from past issues of these magazines on their Web sites, as well as other features that may not appear in the print versions of the magazine.

SEW NEWS
http://www.sewnews.com

THREADS MAGAZINE: THE TAUNTON PRESS
http://www.taunton.com

THREADS MAGAZINE: INDEX OF ARTICLES
http://www.thehudsons.com/threads/threadslasso.html

This site isn't affiliated with Threads, *but it offers what many sewers on the Internet have long been asking for: a searchable index of* Threads *articles and an archive of tables of contents for the magazine. There's also a sale and swap area where you can search for issues you've been wanting to read.*

**Looking for More
Sewing Resources on the Web?**
Visit **Sew City** (**http://www.sewcity.com**), where you'll find
a directory of links to Web sites related to fabric, patterns,
interior design, and more.

Web Sites for Big Sewing Stores

Many of these stores offer free project sheets, sewing tips, and
useful information about the products on their sites.

CALICO CORNERS
http://www.calicocorners.com

JO-ANN'S FABRICS & CRAFTS
http://www.joann.com/index.stm

SEW LAND USA
http://www.sewland-usa.com

FABRIC LAND IN CANADA
http://www.fabriclandwest.com

HANCOCK FABRICS
(MINNESOTA FABRICS/FABRIC WAREHOUSE)
http://www.hancockfabrics.com

Web Sites for Sewing Organizations

AMERICAN SEWING GUILD
http://www.asg.org

HOME SEWING ASSOCIATION & CRAFT ORGANIZATION
http://www.sewing.org

PROFESSIONAL ASSOCIATION OF CUSTOM CLOTHIERS
http://www.paccprofessionals.org

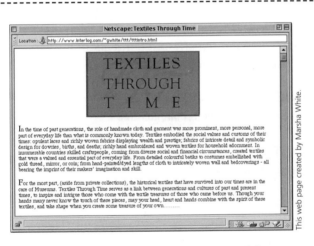

This web page created by Marsha White.

Visit Textile Museums Around the World
Want to tap into the Toronto Museum for Textiles?
How about Auburn University's Macedonian Folk
Embroidery exhibit? Stop in at Marsha White's **Textiles
Through Time (http://www.interlog.com/
~gwhite/ttt/tttintro.html**) for links to all the best textile
museums on the Web.

more Sewers' Coffee Klatches on the Web

S ewers are a convivial bunch. They love to talk to each other. They love to share advice-and of themselves. In Chapters 1 and 2 we describe how to join the cyber-klatches for sewers on America Online and on the big Web sites for sewers. Here is a guide to more special-interest mailing lists and bulletin board discussion groups for sewers.

If you'd like to start your own cyber-club, a number of Web sites let you set up your own e-mail mailing list or bulletin board—for free. What's the catch? An ad might flash on your members' computer screens, but that's about it. Here are our favorite sites to set up a discussion:

DEJANEWS COMMUNITIES
http://www.dejanews.com/communities

ONELIST
http://www.onelist.com

EGROUPS
http://www.egroups.com

By the way, these are also good sites to search for sewing discussions.

 Free Web-based Bulletin Boards and Chats for Sewers

All you need to access these discussion groups is your Web browser.

THE SEWING, QUILTING, AND NEEDLEWORK FORUM
http://www.thathomesite.com/forums/sewing

SEWING WORLD FROM SCOTT AND KRISTA LEWIS
http://www.sewingworld.com

© Krista Lewis, Orchard Studios

THE SEWING BULLETIN BOARD
http://www.wwvisions.com/craftbb/sewing.html

NANCY'S NOTIONS CHAT ROOM
http://www.nancysnotions.com/sewresources.html

HANCOCKS FABRICS' DISCUSSION GROUP
http://www.hancockfabrics.com/bbs.htm

THE THREAD IMAGES MESSAGE BOARD
http://www.threadimages.com/messageboard

THE CRAFTMALL SEWING MESSAGE FORUM
http://www.craftmall.com/forums/sewing

DELPHI'S SEWING SITE FORUM
http://forums.delphi.com/preview/main.asp?sigdir=vysews

DELPHI'S FASHION SEWING GROUP FORUM
http://forums.delphi.com/preview/main.asp?sigdir=fashionsewing

DELPHI'S SEW FRIENDLY FORUM
http://forums.delphi.com/preview/main.asp?sigdir=sew_friendly

**Sewing Mailing Lists Are Fun and Informative,
But You Need to Follow the Rules**
No matter what your interests, mailing lists are your best
source of information on the Internet. But before you sign
up for one, you should read its rules for joining and posting
to the list. Then follow our tips on mailing list netiquette.

- *When you join a mailing list, the computer that
  runs the list will automatically mail you directions
  for participating. Print them and keep them close at
  hand.* Take note of the list's different e-mail addresses.
  You will be sending mail to one address, and sending any
  subscription changes to a different "administrative"
  address. Don't send messages to subscribe or unsubscribe
  to the list to the address that will broadcast your message
  to everyone on the list!

- *You probably have only a limited amount of disk
  space on your ISP to store incoming e-mail. That
  means that if you're a member of a mailing list that
  generates lots of mail, the mail may overrun your
  mailbox if you don't check your e-mail daily.* When
  that happens, e-mail that people send you will bounce
  back to them. And the list may automatically unsubscribe
  you because messages are bouncing back. The solution:
  subscribe to the digest version of the list, if one is available,
  and unsubscribe from the list if you're going out of town.

**VISIT NANCY FOR MAILING LIST
RECOMMENDATIONS**
Nancy Zieman's Web site (**http://www.nancysnotions.com/
sewresources.html**) keeps an up-to-date list of recommended sewing mailing list groups.

The largest sewing discussion mailing list on the Internet is **Sew-L**,
but it's grown so large it's presently closed to new members.

- **If the mailing list has rules about how mail to the list should be addressed, follow them.** Many lists request that members include the list's name in the Subject: line of any messages so that members who have set up their e-mail software to filter messages can do so effectively. You should also try to make the Subject: line of your message as informative as possible for readers who don't have time to read every message posted to the list.

- **Never include your address, phone number, or other personal information in a mailing list post.** Many mailing lists are archived—which means that everyone on the Internet might be able to read them until the end of time!

- **When replying to a message, take a look at the message's address to check where it's going before you hit the Send button.** Don't send a personal reply to everyone on the mailing list. And don't hit Reply to All if the message is addressed to many different people or lists.

 ## Free (and Nearly Free) E-Mail Discussion Groups for Sewers

These are general-interest groups. You'll find more specialized discussion groups in the chapters devoted to their subject matter

WEARABLE ART
To subscribe send an e-mail to: majordomo@embroideryclubs.com. In the Subject: line type *subscribe wearable* or *subscribe wearable-digest*.

THE SEWING CIRCLE
Started by Julie McFann with help from Temple University, this is a general topic sewing discussion group. To join e-mail: listserv@listserv.temple.edu. *In the message type:* sub Sewing-Circle yourname.

THE SEWING LIST
http://www.onelist.com/subscribe.cgi/sewinglist

EGROUPS SEWING GROUPS
http://www.egroups.com

*You'll find several sewing discussion groups on eGroups including one for **Tailoring** and the **Christian Ladies Sewing Group**. You'll need to use the site's search feature to find them.*

THE SUNSHINE GUILD SEWING & CRAFTING
http://adam.cheshire.net/~billijean/index.html

QUILTROPOLIS MAILING LISTS
http://www.quiltropolis.com/NewMailinglists.asp

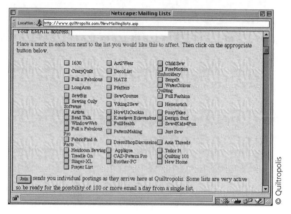

*Quiltropolis hosts over forty needlework mailing lists covering many sewing topics. **Just Sew** is its general-interest sewing discussion group. It's for beginner sewers as well as advanced ones, and you can discuss anything sewing-related on this list.*

***Art2Wear** is for fiber artists, with an emphasis on wearable art. Edie Evans runs the list. Quilters, heirloom sewers, and machine appliqué fans will enjoy the **Appliqué** list, which is for practitioners of both machine and hand appliqué. Quiltropolis also runs several excellent quilting discussion groups including **Quilting 101** and **Crazy Quilt**.*

 Sewing Patterns and Project Sheets

An amazing number of Web sites offer free patterns and sewing project directions. You'll find everything from how-tos for sewing broomstick skirts to stitching up scrunchies and pintucked wastecoats. You'll find patterns for Polar Fleece hats and "bag lady" purses with attitude. So the next time your husband blusters at two a.m., "What are you doing on that computer now?" you can shout back, "I'm printing a pattern for a serged lawnchair cover from the Internet!"

These patterns and project instructions may be free to print or download from the Web, but most are copyrighted by someone. That means that you can stitch them up for yourself or friends, but if you want to reproduce the patterns—in a sewing guild newsletter for example—or sew them to sell them, you need to ask the Web site owner's permission to do so.

THE HOME SEWING ASSOCIATION'S FREE PROJECT ARCHIVE
http://www.sewing.org/project/index.html

PROJECTS FROM BABY LOCK
http://www.babylock.com/projects

PROJECTS FROM ELNA
http://www.elnausa.com/projects/index.htm

PROJECTS FROM JANOME NEW HOME
http://janome.com/projtech.html

PROJECTS FROM PFAFF AUSTRALIA
http://www.pfaffaustralia.com.au/creatcnr.html

PROJECTS FROM VIKING HUSQVARNA
http://www.sew.husqvarna.se/tipen.htm

PROJECTS FROM FAIRFIELD SEW CREATIVE
http://www.fairfieldprocessing.com/crafts/ProjectsAndInfo.html

JENNY'S SEWING PROJECTS
http://jennys-sewing-studio.com/sewproj/1997projects/oldindex.html

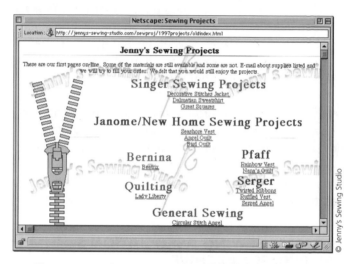

© Jenny's Sewing Studio

Jenny offers projects for specific sewing machines like Janomes, Singers, and Pfaffs, as well as for sergers, but you don't need a special sewing machine to make her projects.

DEBBIE COLGROVE'S FREE SEWING PROJECTS
http://www.angelfire.com/ny/DebbiesPage/freesew.html

SEWING PROJECTS AT ABOUT.COM
http://sewing.about.com

MAKESTUFF.COM'S SEWING CENTER
http://www.makestuff.com/sewing.html

Make a Valentine sweatshirt, a holiday bottle cover, an easy woven ribbon pillow, and more.

ERICA'S FREE PROJECTS LIBRARY
http://www.ericas.com/projects

Erica's Craft & Sewing Center offers instructions for fabric folders, a tucked yoke top, a broomstick skirt, and more. They're available in PDF format, which means you'll need to have **Adobe Acrobat** (**http://www.adobe.com**) *to display them.*

QUILTING FROM
THE HEARTLAND MONTHLY PROJECTS
http://www.qheartland.com/project.htm

MAKE IT EASY: SEWING AND CRAFTS PROJECTS
http://members.xoom.com/make_it_easy/tandt.html

HOUSENET'S SEWING IDEAS
http://www.housenet.com/sw

You'll find a changing selection of projects and ideas from HouseNet, including sewing projects for baby gifts, holiday decorations, and unusual items like crab-eating bibs.

NANCY'S NOTION'S THE SEWING ROOM
http://www.nancysnotions.com/SewingRoomLibrary/Library.html

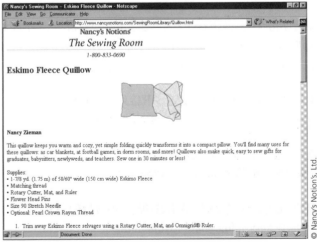

THE BAG LADIES
http://iavbbs.com/jgh/baglady.htm

THE SECRET WORKSHOP
http://www.secretworkshop.com

MR. SEWING'S FREE STUFF
http://www.mrsewing.com.au

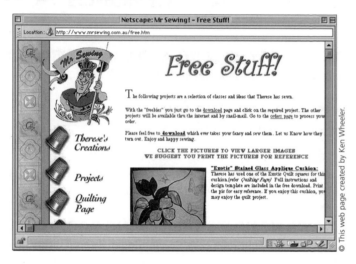

How about stitching up an exotic stained glass applique cushion or that pintucked wastecoat? Theresa and Ken in Queensland, Australia offer a bunch of patterns with downloadable instructions. Click on Mr. Sewing's logo for the free patterns.

JHB INTERNATIONAL'S PROJECT ARCHIVES
http://www.buttons.com/archive/archive.html

CRAFT & SEW ON-LINE
http://www.angelfire.com/id/craftandsew

CINDY CUMMINS' SERGING PROJECTS
http://www.sew-info.com/cindycummins

 Sewing Tips, Tricks, and Hints from Sewers Who've "Been There"

W here do you head on the Internet if you have a basic sewing question? You know, like "How do I finish a pongee seam?" Or, "Is there a good book on sewing for short people?" You can always type your question into a searcher like **Hotbot** (**http://www.hotbot.com**). It might come up with a few applicable Web sites for you, but it won't even skim the surface of all the information for sewers that's out on the Web.

If you have a sewing question, we suggest starting your search by visiting some of the big sewing Web sites we recommend in Chapter 2. You know, like **Nancy Zieman's** Web home (**http://www.nancysnotions.com**)—search the bulletin board areas and Nancy's articles)—or **Sandra Betzina Online** (**http://www.sandrabetzina.com**). Check the forums and Web links at **Delphi's Needlearts** (**http://www0.delphi.com/needle**) and **About.Com's Sewing** (**http://sewing.about.com**) too.

After that, head to the many sewing FAQs, or frequently asked question files, around the Net. These are usually compilations of answers to questions that sewers post in various mailing lists or online forums (though sometimes they're just compilations of one person's opinions).

Frequently Asked Sewing Question Collections

USENET TEXTILE FAQS

The Usenet FAQs are famous compilations of advice that has been posted over the years in the newsgroups **alt.sewing** and the **rec.crafts.textile** ones. They're updated monthly, and you'll find them posted all over the Web, including in each of the newsgroups each month.

The first part of the FAQ covers general sewing questions as well as supply information. It also includes information on restoring antique sewing machines. The second part is about costuming and historical clothing. Another section (divided into three parts, below) lists books that cover sewing, fitting, and pattern drafting.

TEXTILES PART 1 OF 2 - FAQ
ftp://rtfm.mit.edu/pub/usenet/news.answers/crafts/
textiles/faq/part1

TEXTILE PART 2 OF 2 - FAQ
ftp://rtfm.mit.edu/pub/usenet/news.answers/crafts/
textiles/faq/part2

TEXTILE RELATED BOOKS PART 1 OF 3 - FAQ
ftp://rtfm.mit.edu/pub/usenet/news.answers/crafts/
textiles/books/part1

TEXTILE RELATED BOOKS PART 2 OF 3 - FAQ
ftp://rtfm.mit.edu/pub/usenet/news.answers/crafts/
textiles/books/part2

TEXTILE RELATED BOOKS PART 3 OF 3 - FAQ
ftp://rtfm.mit.edu/pub/usenet/news.answers/crafts/
textiles/books/part3

MICHIANA FREE-NET FAQ ABOUT SEWING
http://michiana.org/MFNetLife/SewingFAQ.html

THE SEWING FAQ
http://www.skepsis.com/~tfarrell/textiles/sewing/faq.html

These are alternate sources for the Usenet FAQ material, which can come in handy when the rtfm.mit.edu site is too busy. However, it's best to use the MIT site when you can, since it's always updated promptly.

More FAQs from Other Discussion Groups

THE SEWING LIST FAQ
http://www.jcn1.com/tweedy/collections.html

Lots of information on topics ranging from thread sizes to French darts, sewing satin and velvet, and making Peter Pan collars.

SEWING ROOM SET UP RECOMMENDATIONS
http://www.cheshcat.com/crafts/quilting/q_sewrm.htm

MAIL ORDER RESOURCES FAQ FROM QUILTNET
http://ttsw.com/FAQS/MailOrderFAQ.html

CLOTHING FAQ, COMPILED BY MARK HARRIS FROM VARIOUS NETWORKS
http://www.pbm.com/~lindahl/rialto/clothing-FAQ.html

SEWING BOOK REVIEWS FROM LARA FABANS
http://www.prairienet.org/quilts/sew.books.html

More Web Sites with Oodles of Tips

SEW NEWS MAGAZINE LIBRARY
http://www.sewnews.com/library.htm

JANOME/NEW HOME TECHNIQUES
http://janome.com/projtech.html

"HIDDEN SEAM SECRETS"
BY GAIL BROWN & NANCY ZIEMAN
http://www.nancysnotions.com/SewingRoomLibrary/
HiddenSeamSecrets.html

CHERITH BROOK'S SEWING INFORMATION
http://cherithbrook.tierranet.com/sewinfo.html

THE ECONOMICAL HOMEMAKER:
KEEPING SEWING ECONOMICAL
http://www.thecho.com/sewing.html

NANCY'S SEWING TIPS ARCHIVE
http://tatting.stoneplanet.com/sewtips.asp

ONLINE PAMPHLETS FROM THE
UNIVERSITY OF NEBRASKA EXTENSION
http://www.ianr.unl.edu/pubs/textiles

The Textiles section of the University of Nebraska Extension site is chock-full of articles on all kinds of techniques for sewers, such as lining a jacket or coat, finishing your hem, or different methods of pressing.

free Thrills for Fabriholics

We buy it, collect it, swap it, and protect it like a family treasure: fabric. If you're like most sewers you can't squirrel away enough of it. "She who dies with the most fabric wins," goes the saying. And oh, don't we wish we could take it all with us? There are many Web sites devoted to buying, storing, and using fabric. Chances are that the answer to just about any fabric question you have can be found on the Web.

Quiltropolis (http://www.quiltropolis.com/ NewMailinglists.asp) runs a mailing list discussion group called **FabricFind & Facts**. It's devoted to discussing fiber care, trends in fabrics, and selecting the proper fabric for sewing projects. Judith Gridley is the moderator. They run another discussion group called **Asia Threads** devoted to the appreciation (and acquisition!) of fabrics with Asian roots.

The best collections of fabric advice on the Net can be found in the **QuiltNet FAQs** (QuiltNet is a quilters' discussion group). The **Fabric Storage FAQ (http://www.quilt.com/FAQS/ FabricStorageFAQ.html**) tells you all you need to know about the proper storage of fabric, addressing questions like how to prevent fading and what kind of acid-free boxes to store quilts and heirloom sewing projects in.

The **Bleeding Fabric FAQ (http://ttsw.com/FAQS/ BleedingFabricFAQ.htm**) is a compendium of shared advice on how to determine whether fabrics will bleed, and how to deal with it if they do.

Help for Selecting, Sewing, and Caring for Different Types of Fabric

CRANSTON PRINT WORKS' A BEGINNER'S GUIDE TO FABRICS
http://www.cranstonvillage.com/library/l-f-fabg.htm

Learn how to select fabrics, and learn the difference between fabrics like cambric and chambray, or broadcloth and chino.

FABRIC ADVICE FROM THE UNIVERSITY OF NEBRASKA EXTENSION
http://www.ianr.unl.edu/PUBS/textiles

UNL offers a library of articles on fabric selection, use, and care, many by Rose Marie Tondle.

LABEL TALK
http://www.textileaffairs.com

Ever wonder what those common care symbols and dry-cleaning symbols are all about? The folks at Textile Industry Affairs offer answers, plus stain removal advice.

IOWA STATE UNIVERSITY CLOTHING PUBLICATIONS
http://www.exnet.iastate.edu/Pages/pubs/cl.htm

Documents available for downloading (you need Adobe Acrobat, which is also available to download at the site) include special needs clothing sources, quick and easy stain removal, finding your best fit, and other related topics.

NORTH CAROLINA STATE UNIVERSITY'S "MAINTENANCE AND REPAIR OF TEXTILE AND HOUSE SURFACES"
http://www.ces.ncsu.edu/homecare2/data/hc2.html

"TO WASH OR NOT TO WASH" FROM THIMBLES AND THREAD 🛒
http://threadandthimble.com/wash.htm

If you're sewing a garment you certainly want to launder any fabric before you cut into it—but maybe not if you're stitching a quilt. Read a fascinating collection of messages on the subject.

SEWING WITH SILK
http://www.silkery.com/sewing.html

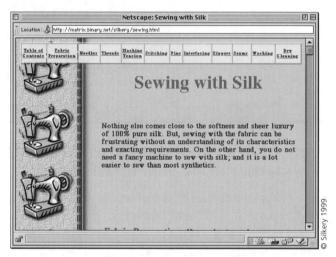

The Silkery offers a guide to sewing silk, including recommendations on the type of needle and thread to use, and cleaning.

APPAREL NET
http://www.apparel.net/index.cgi

You can search this online guide for the apparel industry for special topics and links to other Web resources. Click on the Designers link to get to the web sites of designers like Donna Karan.

PURE WHIMSY
http://www.purewhimsy.com/p354.htm

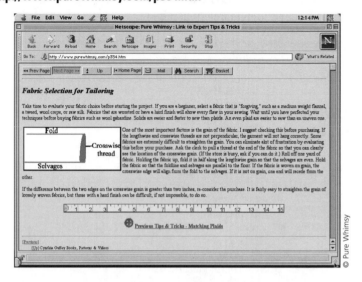

FABRIC ADVICE FROM OHIO STATE UNIVERSITY
http://www.ag.ohio-state.edu/~ohioline/lines/home.html

OSU also offers an extensive library of articles on fabric, many authored by Joyce A. Smith and Barbara Scruggs.

 More Online Stain Removal Guides

STAIN REMOVAL GUIDE
FROM NEW ZEALAND'S KIWI WEB
http://www.chemistry.co.nz/stain.htm

TIDE CLOTHESLINE
http://www.clothesline.com

CLEANING TIPS
FROM SANITARY MAINTENANCE SERVICE, INC.
http://www.sanitarymaintenance.com/cleantp.htm

HOFFMAN CALIFORNIA FABRICS
http://www.hoffmanfabrics.com

Web Sites With Directories of Fabric Retailers, Both On the Web and Off

FABRICS.NET
http://www.fabrics.net

FABRIC STORES LINK FROM SEW CITY
http://www.sewcity.com/sw-fabst.html

SEWSCAPE ONLINE RESOURCE LIST FOR MAIL ORDER AND ONLINE FABRIC
http://www.lyonslpgas.com/sewscape

Looking for Irish dancer's costume fabrics? How about lingerie fabrics? Search the directory of stores on Sewscape.

FABRIC COMPANY DIRECTORY FROM QUILTNET
http://quilt.com/FAQS/FabricCompaniesFaq.html

A list of fabric companies and their addresses, compiled by members.

SEWING SEARCH
http://www.craftsearch.com/Sewing/index.html

You can locate fabric stores by zipcode or name. You can also look up manufacturers.

THE COTTONWORKS FABRIC LIBRARY
http://www.cottoninc.com/FabricLibrary/ccl.cfm

A directory of over three hundred fabric makers with contact information.

FASHIONDEX
http://www.fashiondex.com/apparel/index.vs

Search this directory of manufacturers and retailers of hard-to-find supplies like bridal fabrics, embroideries, silks, fake fur, and more.

Gloria's Tips for Fabric "Power Shopping" on the Web

Face it, shopping for fabric on the Internet simply doesn't compare to shopping for it in person. You can't see it or feel it, and often scans of fabric on Web sites don't match the real thing in color or size of print. But if you're a fabriholic like Gloria, who's never seen a Hoffman print she didn't *have* to buy, you too will soon find yourself tapping your credit card into the Web sites of fabric stores. Here are Gloria's tips for fabric shopping by computer:

- Some fabric stores do a better job of scanning fabric to post on their Web sites than others do. Sometimes the fabric you get in the mail will look very different from what you saw on your computer screen. If you're buying fabric for a project where color and quality are critical, buy swatches first.

- Where should you look for fabric on the Web? Most of the big sewing Web sites (see Chapter 2) offer directories of links to Web sites of fabric stores that sell mail-order. We've listed some directories in the following pages.

SONJA KUEPPERS' LIST OF PLACES TO BUY SILK
http://www.wam.umd.edu/~sek/wedding/silk.html

THE ONLINE FABRIC DIRECTORY
http://www.inetcon.com/fabric

You can search for fabric stores by state—perfect if you are traveling or planning a trip.

- If you see a fabric that you like on the Web site of a fabric manufacturer, print the Web page, and jot down all the details about the fabric (like the name of the company, phone number, bolt number, etc.) and take it to your local fabric store. Some store owners may be willing to order it or track it down for you. Although be warned that not all will do this. (Judy wanted to buy a special fabric from 3M Corp. that the company advertised on its Web site as available at a large national fabric store chain. She printed the Web page and took it to the store. The manager denied knowing anything about the fabric, and insisted the chain didn't carry it. She ended up visiting the store three more times with the copy of the Web page before the manager relented, called the national office, and tracked down the fabric for her.)

- Need yet another reason to splurge on fabric? **Visit 15 Reasons to Buy Fabric (http://www5.palmnet.net/~smith/15reason.htm)** by the Beeline, Utah Quilt Guild. Among the compelling reasons given: It insulates the closet where it is kept and it is cheaper than psychiatric care.

 Web Sites for Major Fabric Makers

What can you find at the Web site of your favorite fabric manufacturer or printer? Lots of good stuff. At Waverly's site, for example, you'll find decorating tips and how-tos for making rooms go along with their fabrics. At Gore-Tex's site you can determine which of their many leading-edge fabrics for outdoor gear is best suited to stitching up that windbreaker. Many of these sites also offer a changing roster of tips and project ideas. They should also be your first stop when you're looking for a retailer of their products in your neighborhood.

BENARTEX
http://www.benartex.com

CHOSEN KNITTERS CO., LTD.
http://www.chosen.com.hk

CRANSTON PRINT WORKS
http://www.cranstonvillage.com

DORR WOOLEN COMPANY
http://www.dorrwoolen.com

GORE-TEX
http://www.gore-tex.com

HOFFMAN CALIFORNIA FABRICS
http://www.hoffmanfabrics.com

THE KIRK COLLECTION
http://www.kirkcollection.com

RJR FASHION FABRICS
http://www.rjrfabrics.com

WAVERLY BRAND
http://www.decoratewaverly.com

P&B TEXTILES
http://www.pbtex.com

CHAPTER 7

 **Advice on Thread,
Notions, and Other
Stuff at the Bottom of
Your Sewing Cabinet**

Think of this as a grab-bag chapter of Web sites where you'll find bits and pieces of advice on the little things that swarm over your sewing table and, like irons and spools of thread, often tumble onto the floor.

 *Web Sites Where You Can Learn
More About Zippers, Buttons, Irons,
and Other Stuff*

SEW-INFO.COM 🚿
http://sew-info.com/OLRG

*Type a word (like "buttonhole" or "serger") into Sew-Info.Com's
searchers and the Web site will display related tips and advice.*

THE ZIPPER PAGE
http://members.aol.com/KALDesign/zipper.html

You'll find these articles here: "Invisible Zippers" by Karen A. Lambert; "Centered Zippers" by Colleen L. Jones; and "Lapped Zippers" by Linda Turcotte.

"LEARN TO FIX A ZIPPER" FROM LEARN2.COM
http://www.learn2.com/04/0462/04624.html

"ADJUSTING THE LENGTH AND WIDTH OF ZIPPERS" FROM THE SECRET WORKSHOP
http://www.secretworkshop.com/Tip5.htm

ROWENTA GARMENT CARE AND IRON RESOURCE CENTER
http://www.rowentausa.com

Learn what iron temperatures to use for different fabrics, and find out what those garment care labels really mean.

NANCY'S NOTIONS—THE BIAS TAPE MAKER
http://nancysnotions.com/SewingRoomLibrary/Tape.html

Nancy Zieman explains how to use a bias tape maker and ways to apply bias tape.

Web Sites Where You Can Learn More About Thread

SEW NEWS' LIBRARY
http://www.sewnews.com/library.htm

Let Sew News *help you tackle thread problems with their thread troubleshooting guide—just one of the many articles you'll find in its library.*

THREAD STORAGE PROJECT
http://members.aol.com/degee2/itdss.htm

Hank and Millie Opel share instructions for a thread storage device, courtesy of Deegee's Digi Designs.

"THREAD FACTS" BY ROSE MARIE TONDL AND WENDY RICH FROM THE UNIVERSITY OF NEBRASKA EXTENSION
http://www.ianr.unl.edu/pubs/NebFacts/NF37.HTM

Did you know you should select thread that's one shade darker than the color you're trying to match? Rose and Wendy fill you in on fiber content, twist, thread types, care, and a whole lot more.

FRANCYNE'S THREAD 101
http://quilt.com/Bernina/Thread101.html

EMBROIDERY THREAD DATABASE
http://www.ud.net/thread

To find a rayon thread color equivalents, enter the color number from Madeira, Pantone, Sulky, etc., and the Web site will display the rayon thread color matches.

 Web Sites of Thread and Notions Makers

Many of these companies offers free advice on using their projects, plus projects and tips on their site. Which of these sites is our favorite? It's a toss-up between Offray's (great ribbon projects) and Fiskars' (great cutting projects).

COATES & CLARK
http://www.coatsandclark.com

DRITZ
http://www.dritz.com

FISKARS SCISSORS
http://www.fiskars.com

GLITZ
http://www.glitz.com

GINGHER SCISSORS
http://www.gingher.com

GUTTERMAN
http://www.guetermann.com

MADERIA
http://www.madeirausa.com

OFFRAY RIBBON
http://www.offray.com

OLFA PRODUCTS
http://www.57thfloor.com/industrial/olfa/home.htm

ROWENTA
http://www.rowentausa.com

SCHMETZ NEEDLES
http://www.schmetz.com

SULKY
http://www.sulky.com

VELCRO
http://www.velcro.com/velcro.htm

free General Sewing Machine Help

We sewers feel as passionate about our sewing machines as car fanciers do for their autos. We polish them; we accessorize them. Some of us even display them. Whether you stitch with a simple Singer or one of the hotrod computerized models, you'll find advice, manuals, and attachments for it on the Net.

We strongly recommend that you join one of the e-mail-based discussion groups for your brand of machine, which you'll find in Chapter 9. The Web sites we recommend in this chapter will get you started buying a sewing machine or serger, troubleshooting basic problems, or fixing up Grandma's treadle. We've even included a Web site that offers advice for drying out a sewing machine that's been soaked by a hurricane.

 ## *Free Sewing Machine Buying Advice*

DEBBIE COLGROVE'S SEWING MACHINE BUYING TIPS AT ABOUT.COM
http://sewing.about.com

"SELECTING A SEWING MACHINE" BY CAROL THAYER
http://ianrwww.unl.edu/pubs/nebfacts/nf110.htm

"SELECTING A SEWING MACHINE" FROM THE HOME SEWING ASSOCIATION
http://www.sewing.org/educate/machine.html

FAQ FOR PURCHASING A SEWING MACHINE, FROM QUILTNET
http://www.quilt.com/FAQS/SewMachinePurchaseFAQ.html

THE USENET TEXTILE FAQ
ftp://rtfm.mit.edu/pub/usenet/news.answers/crafts/textiles/faq/part1

The first part of this frequently asked question file, assembled from messages posted to the textile crafts newsgroups, addresses choices you should consider in buying a machine.

IN THE MARKET FOR A "PREVIOUSLY DRIVEN" SEWING MACHINE?
Visit **Mary Field's Sewing Rummage** (**http://www.jps.net/cfield/rummage**) to read classified ads for second hand sewing machines and accessories. Also, check out the rummage at **eBay** (**http://www.ebay.com**), the Internet flea market where you can find anything old and battered that your heart desires. This is also a great place to hunt for toy sewing machines and sewing machine attachments, especially for vintage models.

Free Help Repairing & Maintaining a Sewing Machine

THE SEW NEWS MACHINE LIBRARY
http://www.sewnews.com/library.htm

This web page created by Missy Shepler and Susan Vougt-Reising for SewNews.

"SEWING MACHINE TROUBLESHOOTING GUIDE" BY SINGER SEWING & VACUUM, NJ

http://www.sewingandvac.com/tshoot.htm

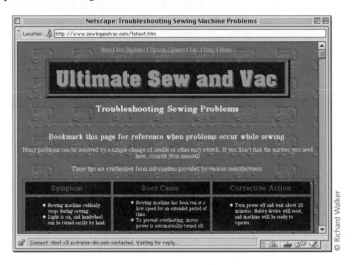

© Richard Walker

"SALVAGING SEWING MACHINES FROM WATER DAMAGE" BY COLLIER (FL) COUNTY EMERGENCY MANAGEMENT

http://www.naples.net/govern/county/emrgmgt/sewing.htm

"WHAT YOU OUGHT TO KNOW ABOUT SEWING MACHINE NEEDLES" BY ROSE MARIE TONDL OF THE UNIVERSITY OF NEBRASKA EXTENSION

http://www.ianr.unl.edu/pubs/NebFacts/nf250.htm

"PUCKERED SEAMS: THE NEEDLE AND THE DAMAGE DONE" BY SANDRA BETZINA

http://www.peekaboo.net/archives/cat13/5.html

Free Help for Lovers of Antique Sewing Machines

TREADLE ON
http://www.quiltropolis.com/NewMailinglists.asp

*This e-mail-based discussion group is hosted by **Quiltropolis** and is dedicated to the use, rather than merely the collection, of treadle and hand-cranked sewing machines.*

FEATHERWEIGHT FANATICS MAILING LIST
http://quilt.com/FWF

Sue Traudt runs this wonderful list for fans of the Singer Featherweight. A modest subscription fee is required.

INTERNATIONAL SEWING MACHINE COLLECTORS SOCIETY
http://www.ismacs.net

"A BRIEF HISTORY OF THE SEWING MACHINE" BY GRAHAM FORSDYKE
http://www.ismacs.net/smhistory.html

The ISMC hosts a mailing list discussion group for collectors of antique machines and offers resources such as links to relevant Web sites.

TANGLED THREADS ANTIQUE SEWING MACHINE FAQ
http://kbs.net/tt/faq/index.html

Melissa Bishop answers the question, "What is a Featherweight anyway?" with historical information, serial number help, plus advice on restoring antique machines.

GAILEE'S FEATHERWEIGHT RESOURCE PAGE
http://www.icsi.net/~pickens

FEATHERWEIGHT FACTS
BY ROB HOLLAND AT PLANET PATCHWORK
http://www.tvq.com/fweight.htm

ALAN QUINN'S ANTIQUE & VINTAGE SEWING MACHINES
http://www.demon.co.uk/quinn

SINGER SEWING COMPANY
INFORMATION I'VE GATHERED
http://www-personal.umich.edu/%7Esherlyn/singer.html

TREADLE ON INFORMATION CENTRAL
http://www.captndick.com

Stop in at the home page of "Captain Dick" Wightman where you can indulge your love of "Treadleonia" with machine information, a cyber-museum of machines, and a flea market of treadle-related stuff.

On the Net, You Can Find Just About Any Sewing Manual Ever Printed
If you're hunting for a manual for that 1942 Singer you hauled in from the neighbor's trash, start your search at **One Stop Shop Singer Sewing Machine Manuals (http://singeronestopshop.com/page4.htm)**. If you discover the machine's not really a Singer but a White, head to **Sewing Manuals, a Look Into the Past (http://www.show.aust.com/~sewing/book.htm)** which sells manuals for any brand of machine. Also keep an eye on **eBay (http://www.ebay.com)** because at any given time there will be fifty or more vintage sewing machine manuals for sale—some selling for less than a spool of thread.

Free Serger Help

QUILTROPOLIS' SERGE IT MAILING LIST
http://www.quiltropolis.com/NewMailinglists.asp

*Thinking of buying a serger? Or looking for ways to expand your
creativity with the one you already have? Sign up for this e-mail-
based discussion group, run by Lili Fischl and Tina Hoak.*

"BUYING A SERGER" BY ROSE MARIE TONDL
AND KATHLEEN HEIDEN AT THE UNIVERSITY
OF NEBRASKA
http://www.ianr.unl.edu/pubs/NebFacts/NF142.HTM

SERGER HELP FROM DEBBIE COLGROVE
AT ABOUT.COM
http://sewing.about.com

LINDA LEE ORIGINALS:
HOME OF THE HAPPY SERGER
http://www.lindaleeoriginals.com

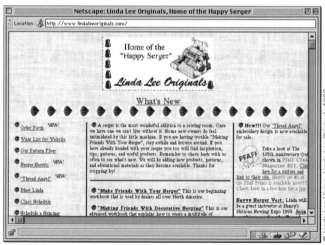

BABY LOCK SERGING HELP
http://www.babylock.com/faqs/faqserg.htm

 Free Help for Industrial Sewing Machines

INDUSTRIAL SEWING MACHINE INFORMATION BY TOPIC
http://www.industrialsewmachine.com/webdoc3.htm

You'll find lots of good—and otherwise hard-to-find—advice here on everything from maintenance to thread.

Planning a Texas Vacation? Visit the World's Biggest Sewing Machine
They do everything big in Texas. Even sewing machines. If you're headed to Arlington stop in at **Frank & Halaina Smith's Sewing Machine Museum** to see a replica of a Civil War sewing machine that's big enough to be a parade float (**http://rampages.onramp.net/~arlprosv/museum.htm**).

Shopping for a Used Industrial Sewing Machine?
Check out the **Sewing Equipment Warehouse** (**http://www.a1sew.com**) which offers a database of new and used industrial machine dealers around the world. They'll link you up with retailers of everything from industrial zig-zag machines to blindstitch and leather stitchers.

 **Help for Specific Brand of Sewing Machines**

J ust as there are computer junkies there are sewing machine nerds. These are sewers who can discourse on the subtleties of the Pfaff's rainbow buttons in their sleep. Or who can troubleshoot problems with a Bernina as fast as old Hans at your sewing machine store. Maybe you're one of them. If so, you'll love the mailing lists and Web sites devoted to your favorite sewing machine.

 ### SEWING WORLD
http://www.sewingworld.com

Krisat Lewis' Sewing World offers a number of bulletin boards to discuss specific models of sewing machines including: Baby Lock, Bernina, New Home, Pfaff, Singer, Viking, Sergers, Brother, and Elna.

 ### BERNINA 1630
http://www.quiltropolis.com/NewMailinglists.asp

Martie Sandell runs this mailing list, sponsored by Quiltropolis, for discussing anything related to the Bernina 1630.

 ### BERNINA USA CHATS AND FORUMS
http://www.berninausa.com/letstalk/index.html

Bernina offers regular online chats with Bernina tech support and marketing people, as well as nationally known Bernina sewing book authors and embroidery design experts. You can also tap into bulletin-board discussions on various related subjects.

Free Help for Berninas

BERNINA FAN CLUB MAILING LIST
http://quilt.com/BFC

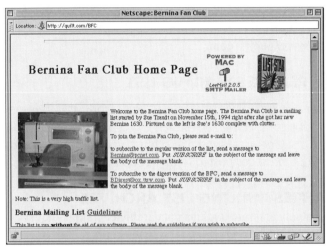

Sue Traudt runs this discussion group, which is popular with quil-ters. From this Web site you can also visit the Web pages of other Bernina fans.

BERNINA QUESTIONS AND ANSWERS
http://www.berninausa.com/qanda/index.html

Bernina offers an easily searchable database of information on their machines.

Free Help for Brother Machines

BROTHER PC MAILING LIST FROM QUILTROPOLIS
http://www.quiltropolis.com/NewMailinglists.asp

Free Help for Pfaffs

 ### SEW-FUN MAILING LIST
http://www.onelist.com/viewarchive.cgi?listname=sew-fun

*You can read this mailing list for "dinosaur" Pfaffs through a bulletin board or e-mail. It's run through **Onelist** (http://www.onelist.com).*

 ### PFAFFIES MAILING LIST

To join this discussion group e-mail: majordomo@embroideryclubs.com. In the Subject: line of the message type subscribe. In the message type: subscribe pfaffies yourfullname. You can read past messages posted to the group by heading to:

PFAFFIES MAILING LIST ARCHIVES
ftp://listserv.embroideryclubs.com/archives/pfaffies-digest

 ### PFAFFERS
http://www.quiltropolis.com/NewMailinglists.asp

This list, run by Pandy Lolos and Susan Druding, is for owners of the 1475, 7550, and 7570 machines. This list is for busy sewers and has strict rules about no chatting or off-topic messages. Using the PC Design software to design embroidery is a focus of the list.

 ### MARY FIELD'S PFAFF SEWING ROOM PFAFFPFRIENDS MAILING LIST AND ARCHIVES
http://www.jps.net/cfield/pfaff

Check out Mary Field's sewing room and subscribe to the Pfaffpfriends mailing list and read archives of their messages.

PAULA MILNER'S SEWING AND DACHSHUNDS
http://www.cyberport.net/users/milnerwm

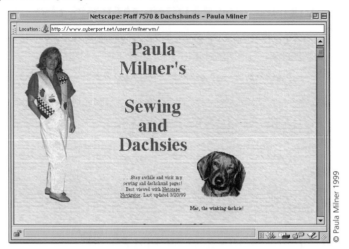

PAULA MILNER'S PFAFFIE FAQ
http://www.cyberport.net/users/milnerwm/FAQ.html

You'll find information and links to resources around the Net to answer just about every question you have about your Pfaff. This is a wonderful site!

 ## PFAFF-TALK BULLETIN BOARD
FOR NON-HOOP MACHINES
http://www.pfaff-talk.com/non-hoop_machines

PFAFF-TALK BULLETIN BOARD
FOR HOOP MACHINES LIKE THE 7570
http://www.pfaff-talk.com/hoop_machines

Free Help for Singer Machines

SINGER XL MAILING LIST
http://www.quiltropolis.com/NewMailinglists.asp

Quiltropolis runs a discussion group for Singer owners.

Free Help for Viking Machines

 ## VIKING VENERATIONS MAILING LIST

To join this chatty group of Viking owners e-mail:
majordomo@acpub.duke.edu.
Don't put anything in the subject line. In the message type:
subscribe viking-l. *That's an "L" as in Linda.*

VIKING2SEW MAILING LIST
http://www.quiltropolis.com/NewMailinglists.asp

Robin Elder runs this mailing list sponsored by Quiltropolis and devoted to discussing Viking sewing machines, sergers, embroidery, customizing and digitizing.

KNOW YOUR VIKING NEEDLES
http://www.lydias.com/needle3ainfo.html

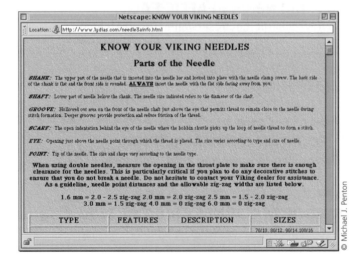

D. Hoeflinger from Lydia's Heirloom Sewing discusses different types of machine needles.

THREADS MAGAZINE REVIEW OF THE VIKING #1
http://www.taunton.com/th/features/techniques/5viking.htm

 Free Help for New Home/Janome Machines

JANOME NEW HOME FAQ
http://janome.com/faq.html

Sewing-machine maker Janome answers questions such as, "When I try to sew a blind hem, I always see too much of my thread in the front of my garment. How can I make smaller stitches?"

HINTS & TIPS FOR NEW HOME/JANOME SEWING MACHINES
http://www.sewingroom.com/tiphdr.htm

Stutsman and The Sewing Room offer lots of help, including information on the Scan 'n Sew PC.

 ### JANOME NEW HOME MAILING LIST FROM QUILTROPOLIS
http://www.quiltropolis.com/NewMailinglists.asp

Web Sites of Sewing Machine Makers

Many manufacturers offer tips, project pages, and extensive resources and information about their machines on their Web sites.

BABY LOCK CANADA
http://www.babylockcanada.com

BERNINA
http://www.berninausa.com

ELNA USA
http://www.elnausa.com

BROTHER
http://www.brother.com

HUSQVARNA VIKING
http://www.husqvarnaviking.com

JANOME NEW HOME
http://www.janome.com

JUKI
http://www.juki.com

MELCO
http://www.melco.com

PFAFF
http://www.pfaff.com

PFAFF AUSTRALIA
http://www.pfaffaustralia.com.au

RICCAR
http://www.riccar.com

SINGER
http://www.singersewing.com

BABY LOCK
http://www.babylock.com

 Help and Designs for Machine Embroidery

Whether you occasionally dabble in free-motion embroidery with an ordinary sewing machine or own a dedicated embroidery machine with a digitizer, there are Web sites that will help with designs, advice, and even software. In fact, there are so many Web sites for machine embroiderers one might conclude that there are few people on the Internet who *don't* machine embroider. (Actually, we're beginning to wonder about that.) We can offer only a sampling of sites. We've chosen ones that we think will provide you with basic answers to questions about your machine, plus connect you with other embroidery enthusiasts. And as we like to remind you, other sewers are always your best source for any kind of information on the Net.

 ## *Free Discussion Groups for Machine Embroiderers*

✋ Many of the e-mail discussion groups listed in Chapter 9 are populated with ardent machine embroiderers. We suggest joining a group devoted to your sewing machine and using that as your primary resource in finding answers to your questions about embroidering with your specific machine.

FREEMOTIONS
http://www.quiltropolis.com/NewMailinglists.asp

Beth Ober of Quiltropolis runs this e-mail list, dedicated to discussing free-motion embroidery as opposed to designing or using a sewing machine's pre-programmed embroidery stitches. In free-motion embroidery you disengage the feed dogs and use a darning foot to fill in areas of fabric with straight or zigzag stitches. You guide the stitching by hand or by "free motion."

HUSQVIKING ARTISTRY THROUGH SEWING (HATS)
http://www.quiltropolis.com/NewMailinglists.asp
http://207.222.205.33/hatsmain.html#Welcome to HATS

*Lili Fischl and Tina Hoak run this list through Quiltropolis, for own-
ers of the souped-up Husqvarna Viking #1+, Rose, #1, 500, or
1100. The focus of the list is on using the machines for embroidery and heirloom sewing, with special emphasis on digitizing and
using the software to design.*

ARTISTA
http://www.quiltropolis.com/NewMailinglists.asp

*If you have the Bernina 170/180 and/or Artista
Customizer/Designer Software this mailing list through Quiltropolis
is for you.*

BROTHER BABYLOCK DECO MAILING LIST
http://members.aol.com/Cmonsterx/bbdlist.htm

*To join this lively group, send a message to:
majordomo@listserv.embroideryclubs.com. In the body of the
message type:* subscribe bbd.embroidery-digest, *or head to the
above Web page for directions. Cookie Gaynor offers the **Best of
the BBD Mailing List** (**http://members.aol.com/Cmonsterx
/home.htm**) as well as a message board at her Web site.*

DECOLIST
http://www.quiltropolis.com/NewMailinglists.asp

*This group, run by Martie Sandell and hosted by Quiltropolis, is for
owners of the Brother-made standalone embroidery machine,
whether you own the scanner or not. Beginners are welcome, as
are advanced users.*

PFAFFPFRIENDS
http://www.onelist.com/subscribe.cgi/pfaffpfriends

This group is devoted to discussing the Pfaff 7570 and its embroidery features, although any machine embroiderer is welcome to join.

TASHAMBRA'S SEWING & EMBROIDERY TALES MAILING LIST
http://www.tashambra.com/sewing_embroidery_mailing_list.htm

"If you are tired of not being able to stray off topic on all the other mailing lists you are on, then come join us," writes Tashambra. Discussion of any type of sewing or embroidery machine is welcome on her list.

THE MACHINE EMBROIDERY CLUB AT YAHOO
http://clubs.yahoo.com/clubs/machineembroidery

A Web-based bulletin board for owners of Pfaff, Brother, Viking, and New Home machines, run by "TBearWoman" a.k.a. Mary Jane from Williamsburg, Virginia.

EMBJAZZCHAT
EMBJAZZDBD
http://www.jazzerstitches.com

Julie Rueckheim of Jazzerstitches runs two mailing lists. EMBjazzchat is for sewers who own any kind of home embroidery machine. EMBjazzDBD (Digitizing by Design) is for owners of Brother, Babylock, and Bernina Deco machines and software.

MACHINE EMBROIDERY LIST - BBD

This e-mail list is for owners of Brother, Babyloc, or Deco embroidery machines. To join e-mail: majordomo@embroideryclubs.com. In the message type: subscribe bbd.embroidery your_email_address

TRAVEL THE RING OF STITCHES WEB RING TO VISIT THE WEB SITES OF MACHINE EMBROIDERERS

Elaine Rieck runs a Web ring that connects over a hundred Web sites of machine embroidery fans (**http://members.home.net/erieck/form.htm**). *You don't have to "join" the ring in order to surf it. Merely scroll down the page and select List sites to see the complete list.*

 Web Sites that Offer
General Machine Embroidery Tips

LINDEE GOODALL'S MACHINE EMBROIDERY GLOSSARY
http://www.sewnews.com/library/mach6.htm

Lindee explains all the terms from "back appliqué" to underlay stitch in this article from Sew News.

TENSION CHECK DESIGN
http://www.tropicalpunch.com/tension.html

Tropical Punch offers downloadable designs and instructions for checking the thread tension of your machine.

EMBROIDERY PLACEMENT GUIDELINES
http://www.embroiderymall.com/library/placement.html

Where you place your design on the fabric can make a big difference in its appearance. Big Bear offers a guide to where to place designs on golf shirts, T-shirts, turtlenecks, bath towels, pockets, cuffs, and more.

 # Web Sites that Offer Help with Machine Embroidery Software

"A FEW PERSONAL OPINIONS ABOUT EMBROIDERY SOFTWARE" BY ANNE PYLE
http://www.thelilispad.com/pages/Softwarecomparison.htm

ROSEMARY ROSENBLUM'S GUIDE TO EMBROIDERY FILE EXTENSIONS
http://hometown.aol.com/rrosebud13/FilExt.htm

EXXXTERMINATOR FILE SOFTWARE
http://members.aol.com/_ht_a/beacoqui/main/programs.htm

Rudolf and Bea Coqui offer a program for converting between different embroidery file formats, including DST, PCS, PES, SEW, and others.

BUZZ TOOLS
http://buzztools.com

With Buzz Tools software you can display embroidery design files and convert them from one format to another.

Web Sites that Offer Advice on Embroidering with Specific Machines

PAULA MILNER'S PFAFFIE FAQ
http://www.cyberport.net/users/milnerwm/FAQ.html

Visit Paula's Web site when you have any question whatsoever about embroidering with a Pfaff. She offers everything from digitizing lessons to thread help, to links to software and free embroidery designs that you can download.

ELAINE'S CREATIVE DESIGN TIPS & TRICKS
http://members.home.net/erieck/tips.htm

Elaine's is another great resource for Pfaffies using Creative Design. She offers tutorials on such wide-ranging topics as how to reformat your Creative Design Glank Card, how to outline a digitized design by using corner stitches, how to position your design with the Pfaff 7570 embroidery hoop, how to deal with metallic thread and stabilizers, and oh so much more!

ARTISTA TIPS & TRICKS
FROM RAINBOWS END EMBROIDERY
http://www.rainbowsendembroidery.com/ArtistaTips.htm

You'll find a huge archive of tutorials for embroidery design assembled from contributions of Artista fans around the Net.

Are You Trying to Run PC Embroidery Software on Your Mac?
One way to do it is with MacDOScard, and if you want to know how, join the MacDOScard Mailing List (**http://saratoga.tmnet.com.my/macdoscard**).

Stuff to Help with Pfaff Creative Designer Software

ELAINE RIECK'S GUIDE TO PFAFF CREATIVE DESIGNER PROGRAMS
http://members.home.net/erieck/pcdutil.htm

Reviews and Web links to sources on the Net for add-on programs to use with Pfaff's PC Designer.

SUZANNE LANE'S TIPS & TRICKS
http://www.isn.net/~dlane/tips.html

Suzanne, a Pfaff dealer, offers lots of help with using the PC Designer software.

GLYNDA BLACK'S DESIGNS
http://starflight.com/gbdesigns

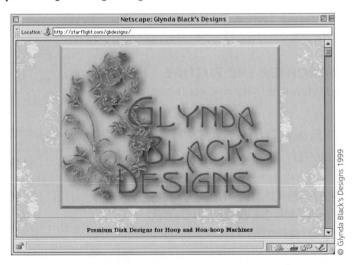

Glynda offers tips for using Pfaff Creative Designer software.

PAULA MILNER'S LINKS TO PFAFF SOFTWARE
http://www.cyberport.net/users/milnerwm/FAQ.html

Paula offers links to many programs for Pfaff sewers.

XSTITCH
http://privat.swol.de/ulitessel/english.html

*Uli Tessel of Germany wrote a program to allow his mother to create cross-stitch designs for Pfaffs. He made it available for free on the Net, and it's become a hit with Pfaff users. After you download it read Phyllis's tutorial on using it at **Phyllis's Machine Embroidery Page** (http://www.PhylliStitch.com/cross.htm).*

KWIK-DRAW AND TRANSFER SOFTWARE
http://members.aol.com/_ht_a/beacoqui/main/programs.htm

Rudolf and Bea Coqui offer software for transferring multiple files from a PC, running PC Designer to a Pfaff 7570 memory card, and a program for creating PCS files from geometric shapes.

 Free Stuff to Help with Husqvarna

TIPS AND TRICKS FROM THELILI'SPAD
http://www.thelilispad.com/pages/tipsandtricks.htm

EMBROIDER THE FUTURE
http://www.embroiderynetworks.com/html

 Free Stuff to Help with New Home/Janome

TIPS FOR USING SCAN 'N SEW PC FROM THE SEWING ROOM
http://www.sewingroom.com/tiphdr.htm

Diane Stutsman even tells you how to use it with a Macintosh.

Web Sites that Offer Free Machine Embroidery Designs

There are many, many Web sites that offer free embroidery designs that you can download and use with your Pfaff, Viking, Janome, or other home sewing or embroidery machine.

First you need to know what file format your machine uses. (Most Pfaffs use .PCD or .PCQ. The .PES format is used by Babylock, Deco, Brother, Bernette, and Esante. Vikings use .HUS. Janomes use .SEW.) You also need to know how to transfer or "download" the design from your computer to your sewing or embroidery machine once you snag it off a Web site. (If you're a Pfaffer read the following tutorial from the Pfaffies mailing list, supplied by Paula Milner at **http://www.cyberport.net/users/milnerwm/FAQ/DLandSEW**.)

Remember that the embroidery designs you find on the Web are copyrighted. You should not embroider them on items that you plan to sell without obtaining permission from the copyright owner. Keep in mind too that some Web sites have been known to distribute embroidery designs that belong to someone else, and which they should not have posted as "free" on their site. In other words, not everyone is savvy about copyright laws.

Finally, we recommend running these embroidery design files through a virus checker after you download them and before you load them in your embroidery design software.

"HATSWAP" FROM THE HATS (HUSKVIKING ARTISTRY THROUGH SEWING) MAILING LIST
http://207.222.205.33/hatswap.html#HATSWAP

The members of HATS share lovely embroidery designs through this site maintained by Kitty Vickers.

🛒 Some of these sites offer free embroidery designs in multiple formats, while others concentrate on just one—Pfaff PCD, for example, or Viking HUS. This is just a small sampling of what's available, to get you started. Keep exploring on your own, and remember that discussion lists are usually the best place to find out about more designs.

ARTISTA DESIGN EXCHANGE
http://www.goingsewing-artista.com

This Web page created by Reneah D. Raffay.

ANN THE GRAN'S DESIGN EXCHANGE
http://www.annthegran.com

BUBBLE'S MENAGERIE BY LISA SHAW
http://www.sewdesigns.com/bubbles

THREAD IMAGES
http://www.threadimages.com

FREEBIES TO DOWNLOAD
FROM DEEGEE'S DIGI DESIGNS
http://members.aol.com/degee/freebies.htm

DEBBIE'S DESIGN EXCHANGE
http://www.angelfire.com/hi/debbiedesigns

THE EMBROIDERY EXPERIENCE, INC.
http://www.stitchbyte.com/service.html

FREE EMBROIDERY DESIGNS
FROM ERICA'S SEWING AND CRAFT CENTER
http://www.ericas.com/freedesigns/

ELAINE'S DESIGN GALLERY
http://members.home.net/erieck/pcs.htm

ZARI'S SEWING HOME PAGE
http://www.interworx.com.au/users/zari/index.htm

EMBROIDERY FREEBIES
http://www.ziplink.net/users/sewbev/embroidery_freebies.htm

PFAFF DESIGNS FROM RALF FRIEDRICH
http://www.friedrich.org/pcs

CATHERINE'S STITCH IN THYME
http://www.qis.net/~cpaulson/

THE DESIGN DEN
http://members.aol.com/sewnquilt/en/den.htm
http://members.aol.com/sewnquilt/archive/archive.htm

FREE DESIGNS
FROM JUDY'S EMBROIDERY HAVEN
http://www.sewdesigns.com/Judys/EmbroideryHaven/free.html

SHERRI'S SEWING AND DIGITIZING FREEBIES
http://members.aol.com/SEWMANI03/Freebies.html

SUSAN'S SEWING CORNER
http://www.delanet.com/~struitt

TRAVEL THE FREE EMBROIDERY DESIGNS WEB RING

You can surf a ring of connected Web sites of machine embroidery junkies who offer free embroidery

designs on their sites by heading to: **http://www.tashambra.com/ web_ring.htm.** *You don't have to "join" the ring in order to surf it. Simply click on the "Next" link.*

PFABULOUS PFREE
PFANTASY PFAFF SHAREGROUND
http://www.SewDesigns.Com/derosia

You'll find thousands of free designs donated from people from around the world at this site maintained by John & Sherry DeRosia.

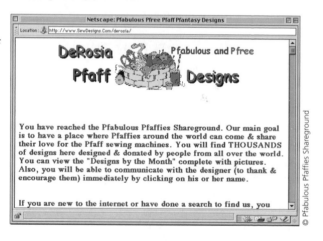

Many of the sewing machine mailing list discussion groups described in this and the previous chapters maintain archives of free embroidery designs that members have shared. To find out more, join a discussion list.

CHAPTER 11

free Help Finding Hard-to-Find and Vintage Patterns

One of the most common questions we hear from sewers is, "Is there some way I can find an out-of-print sewing pattern on the Web?" Debbie Colgrove, the sewing guide at the About.Com, has done considerable research into this and discovered that many of the major pattern publishers, including Butterick, Simplicity, and Vogue will search their old inventory for specific patterns if you give them a call. She offers phone and e-mail contact information for them among her features at the **About.Com Sewing Forum (http://sewing.about.com/library/weekly/aa081498.htm**), where she also maintains an up-to-date directory of Web sites of specialty pattern companies.

There are also bulletin boards around the Net where you can post requests for the patterns you're hunting. But we think that the odds that someone who has the pattern will see your message are about even with finding intelligent life in another galaxy through smoke signals. However, there are a number of Web sites that sell discontinued patterns, and we've included a list of them in the following pages.

At the risk of sounding like a broken record, we highly recommend the Web flea market **eBay (http://www.ebay.com**) as a terrific place to search for old patterns and magazines. Every pattern ever printed will probably find its way onto eBay at some point. You need to check the service daily because auction offerings change so quickly, and see page 170 for our tips on shopping at cyber flea markets.

🛒 Web Sites that Sell Vintage and Discontinued Sewing Patterns

BEKI'S SEWING PATTERNS
http://www.sewingpatterns.com

Beki sells all sorts of clothing patterns. Among her ever-changing inventory you'll find Gunne Sax and Laura Ashley patterns, apron patterns, and Brooke Shields' patterns (remember those?), as well as patterns from all the major pattern companies. And if you have old patterns you want to get rid of, Beki's buying.

PATTERNS FROM THE PAST
http://www.oldpatterns.com

This Web store offers a wonderful selection of old patterns, including wedding gowns and costume patterns. It also runs a vintage sewing patterns club through Yahoo.

KAYE'S FASHION & SEWING ONLINE
http://www.mat.net/~krisna/index.html

Kaye sells vintage clothing patterns that range from cocktail dresses to old Woman's Day Wear patterns. She sells vintage embroidery transfers, too.

LILY ABELLO'S VINTAGE PATTERN SHOP
http://www.lilyabello.com/patternshop

You can shop by decade—from the '20s to the '70s—for Vogue, McCall's, Butterick, Simplicity, and other patterns.

RUSTYZIPPER.COM
http://www.rustyzipper.com

It's not easy to browse—you have to know what you're looking for and use each store's search engine, but this vintage clothing Web site offers a large selection of patterns.

HARD TO FIND NEEDLEWORK BOOKS
http://www.needleworkbooks.com

Bette S. Feinstein doesn't sell sewing patterns, but she offers a large variety of books—and old magazines like Sew News, Threads, *and* Sewing Basket. *She'll also search for out-of-print needlework books for you.*

✊ If you're thinking of buying vintage sewing patterns keep in mind that vintage sizes rarely have any relation to modern sizing. For instance, a Size 10 coat pattern from the '50s will probably not fit a modern Size 10, but may be better suited for a Size 3! Always ask the seller if the pattern package specifies body measurements. If you wind up with the wrong size, don't be disappointed. Remember how your home-ec teacher in high school showed you how to tape and pin the pattern pieces to your body—while you are discretely wearing a dress slip!—and enlarge them where necessary (usually around the hips).

🛒 Web Sites that Sell Reproductions of Vintage Patterns

There are many, many Web sites where you can buy reproductions of old patterns and historical garb. We couldn't list them all, but you'll find more at Julie Zetterberg's **The Costume Page** (**http://members.aol.com/nebula5/costume.html**). Also, head to Chapter 25, Free Stuff for Costumers, for more pattern links.

AMAZON DRYGOODS
http://amazondrygoods.com

MILLER'S MILLINERY
http://bonnets.com

PAST PATTERNS
http://www.pastpatterns.com

HARPER HOUSE
http://www.longago.com

🛒 Web Sites of Major Pattern Publishers

Though the Web sites of major pattern makers tend to be austere on freebies, they do offer occasional features and good advice on stitching up their patterns. They're also great places to check out upcoming patterns and styles.

BUTTERICK
http://www.Butterick.com

BURDA
http://www.glpnews.com/Crafts.html

FOLKWEAR
http://www.larkbooks.com

KWIK SEW
http://www.kwiksew.com

MCCALL'S
http://www.mccall.com

SIMPLICITY
http://www.simplicitypatt.com

STRETCH & SEW
http://www.stretch-and-sew.com

VOGUE
http://www.VoguePatterns.com

🛒 Web Sites of Up-and-Coming Pattern Publishers

THE PARK BENCH PATTERN COMPANY
http://www.sewnet.com/parkbench

"Clothing for soft, easy, comfortable dressing." Patterns are non-tailored, come in a wide range of sizes, and have lots of areas for surface design.

PEGGY SAGERS & SILHOUETTE PATTERNS
http://www.getcreativeshow.com/peggy_sagers.htm

Peggy sells patterns that come with fitting for B, C, and D cup sizes.

SEW GRAND PATTERNS
http://www.sewgrand.com

High-fashion patterns for large sizes

 Help for Sewing
Hats and Outerwear

Nothing brightens your face like a stylish jabot. But why stop at a hat? Why not sew a coat to go along with it? Sewing coats is not hard. In fact, once you sew one you'll be addicted. (The hard part is finding coat fabrics and linings.) Why schlep through stores hunting for a new coat when one is as close as an afternoon at the sewing machine—and on the Web!

 Help for Sewing Hats

MILLINERY BASIC STITCHES
http://www.teasociety.com/victorian/millinery/millcurric1.html

Shenlei E. Winkler and The Victorian Fashion Pages offer hand-stitching help for hat makers.

HOW TO TIE A TURBAN USING 2 CONTRASTING TASSEL SCARVES
http://www.greatbasin.net/~caravan/turban.htm

If you've ever suffered a bad hair day—or one of those days with no hair at all, you'll appreciate the ability to give yourself a new headdress with a few scarves and a knot or two.

HOME SEWING ASSOCIATION PATTERN FOR CHEMOTHERAPY TURBANS
http://www.sewing.org/careshare/turban.html

The HSA offers complete directions for turbans for different head sizes, plus advice on how your sewing guild can sew them in an assembly line fashion.

COMFORT CAPS CANCER HAT PROJECT
http://www.sewing.org/careshare/comfortcap.html

Learn about this charity for sewing soft and fashionable hats for cancer patients. They offer a free pattern, although it's not available online.

"MAKE YOUR OWN HAT FROM 'TITANIC' OR 'WINGS OF THE DOVE'" BY DAVYNE DIAL
http://www.Davynedial.com/cinema_hat_instructions.html

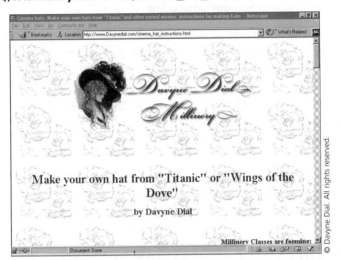

An expert milliner gives instructions for whipping up reproduction of vintage ladies' hats from the movies.

PATTERN FOR A 16TH CENTURY ENGLISH SLOUCH HAT, BY "M. RONDALLYNN OF GOLGOTHA"
http://www.mtsu.edu/~kgregg/dmir/09/0915.html

Help for Sewing Outerwear

"MAKING OUTERWEAR WITH DOWN OR POLYSTER FIBERFILL" BY SUSAN WRIGHT, FROM THE NEW MEXICO STATE UNIVERSITY EXTENSION
http://www.cahe.nmsu.edu/pubs/_c/c-230.html

GEAR AID ONLINE REPAIR MANUAL
http://www.gearaid.com/manual.htm

Get advice on sewing your hiking and mountaineering gear. Find out how to use grommets and adhesive patches to make repairs, fixing sleeping pads and tent poles, and more.

"SEWING AND CARING FOR MICROFIBER" BY SANDRA BETZINA
http://www.peekaboo.net/archives/cat13/32.html

TIPS FOR SEWING WITH POLAR FLEECE
http://www.deelightful.com/fleece.htm

SUITABILITY EQUESTRIAN PATTERNS
http://www.suitability.com

Want to sew your own riding wear? SuitAbility sells a wide range of patterns ranging from English riding coats to western wear, for both adults and children. They also sell patterns for saddle bags, feed bags, hat-carrying bags, and other equestrian accessories. Their Web site offers tips, materials and source information, a book on sewing riding clothes, and more.

For more information on selecting, sewing, and caring for the many different high-tech outdoor gear fabrics head to Chapter 6, Free Thrills for Fabriholics.

 Help Sewing Lingerie That Really Fits

Face it, they never fit right. You know what we're talking about. Their straps cut into your shoulders. Their elastic reddens your back. You're not the average woman if you've never dreamed that your bra is suffocating you. There are many sites on the Web devoted to exploring the subtleties of stitching the perfect bra; so many it astounded us. There are even Web sites where you can buy bra hardware.

UNDERWIRE AND BRAS FAQ
http://www.funhouse.com/babs/FAQ.html

If you're thinking of sewing your own the first thing to do is read this famous FAQ from the Usenet newsgroup rec.crafts.textiles.sewing. It will tell you all you need to know to fashion a bra, where to buy notions and supplies for bras, how to fit bras and a discussion of fabrics for bras. You'll also find a link to related FAQs on the history of undergarments and clothing for large people.

BASIC BRA INSTRUCTIONS
http://home1.gte.net/diannegl/Basic%20Bra.html

Dianne Gleaton teaches the basic techniques for sewing bras.

"THE BRA DILEMMA SOLVED!" BY CINDY ELAM FOR THREADS
http://www.taunton.com/th/features/fitandfabric/bra/page1.htm

"BRAS FOR MASTECTOMY" BY CINDY ELAM FOR THREADS
http://www.taunton.com/th/features/techniques/46bra.htm

BUST CUP SEWING PATTERN ENLARGEMENT
http://web0.tiac.net/users/fancyth/bustadjust.htm

Colleen L. Jones compiled this information from the **Full and Fabulous** mailing list—which you can read more about at **Quiltropolis** (**http://www.quiltropolis.com**).

CORSETRY
http://www.waisted.com

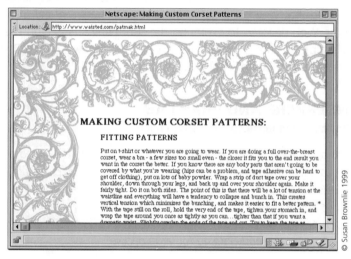

© Susan Brownlie 1999

Why anyone would want one is beyond us. But if you do, Susan Brownlie offers illustrated instructions for everything you need to know to make a corset.

"HOW TO MAKE A COTTON HALF SLIP" FROM RINA'S SEWING PAGE
http://www.gl.umbc.edu/~rabzug1/sewing/slip.html

Head to **Sew Sassy** for a selection of bra-making hardware (**http://www.SewSassy.com/BraProducts/Closures.html**).

 # Tailoring, Fitting, and Pattern-Drafting Help

F ace it, the patterns you buy in the store bear little relation to physical reality. We all have arms that are too long or too thick, tummies that protrude, shoulders that would burst out of a football player's uniform, or calves that make the prospect of buying off-the-rack pants that fit a laughable proposition. There is no such thing as a standard body shape, although pattern publishers and the garment industry might like us to think otherwise. Adjusting patterns to fit and stitching garments that hang in a flattering manner is one of the great challenges of sewing—unless you're like us and stick to wearing bathrobes and kimonos most of the time. Fortunately there are many Web sites that will help you with sewing clothes that fit, or at least get you started in the right direction. We've even included a Web site that will teach you how to make a dressmaker's dummy out of duct tape!

 ### TAILOR IT MAILING LIST
http://www.quiltropolis.com/NewMailinglists.asp

A mailing list on tailoring, for beginners and advanced sewers.

 ### SEWCOUTURE MAILING LIST
http://www.quiltropolis.com/NewMailinglists.asp

Another excellent discussion group run by Quiltropolis—this one is for advanced sewers who are interested in discussing issues of couture design and construction. List members discuss sewing bridal and formal wear, too.

GET CREATIVE
http://www.getcreativeshow.com/Crafting_Sewing_Conference_
Center/craft_sewing_seminars.htm

*This site offers lots of articles on tailoring including ones on fitting
pants, correcting a choking neckline, choosing patterns that fit,
and tips for using multi-sized patterns.*

"FIT & FABRIC" FROM THREADS ONLINE
http://www.taunton.com/th/admin/fitandfabric.htm

*Threads magazine offers a marvelous selection of fitting how-tos
like "Stop! Are You Sure That Pattern Will Work?"*

"FITTING SURPRISES" BY SANDRA BETZINA
http://www.peekaboo.net/archives/cat13/4.html

"MULTI-SIZE PATTERNS CAN MAKE YOU LOOK
GOOD" BY SANDRA BETZINA
http://www.peekaboo.net/archives/cat13/8.html

 Free Pattern-Drafting Help

 PATTERNMAKING MAILING LIST
http://www.quiltropolis.com/NewMailinglists.asp

*This e-mail discussion group from Quiltropolis is devoted to help-
ing members learn the art of drafting their own patterns.*

Thinking of trying pattern drafting software? Head to
Chapter 24 for the addresses of Web sites where you can
download demos and get advice on using the different programs. Visit the Web sites of major pattern makers listed in
Chapter 11 for pattern fitting and measuring advice.

Free Pants Fitting Help

"THE PANT STORY" BY SANDRA BETZINA
http://www.peekaboo.net/archives/cat13/1.html

"FITTING OVER A TUMMY"
BY SANDRA BETZINA
http://www.peekaboo.net/archives/cat13/16.html

"TAPERING OR WIDENING PANTS"
FROM THREADS ONLINE
http://www.taunton.com/th/features/fitandfabric/2tapering.htm

"WALKING ROOM IN PANTS"
FROM THREADS ONLINE
http://www.taunton.com/th/features/fitandfabric/12walkingroom.htm

 Free Help Fitting Large Sizes

 ## FULL AND FABULOUS MAILING LIST
http://lyris.quiltropolis.com/scripts/lyris.pl?enter=fullfab
http://www.quiltropolis.com/NewMailinglists.asp

Gail Dennis runs this discussion group through Quiltropolis. "The purpose of this list is to help men and women get past the weight and feel good about themselves by creating beautiful, stylish clothes that will compliment their figure." she writes. Topics include image type, colors, pattern adjustments, sewing challenges, self-esteem, and fashion hints.

 ## FULL AND FABULOUS PRO MAILING LIST
http://www.quiltropolis.com/NewMailinglists.asp *or*
e-mail: FullFabJoinInfo@lyris.quiltropolis.com.

This discussion group, also run by Gail Dennis, is a "no-nonsense, no-chat" list for advanced sewers. There is a modest yearly subscription fee.

FULL FASHION MAILING LIST
http://www.quiltropolis.com/NewMailinglists.asp

"CLOTHING FOR BIG FOLKS FAQ" FROM OHIO STATE UNIVERSITY
http://www.cis.ohio-state.edu/hypertext/faq/usenet/fat-accept-ance-faq/clothing/us/faq.html

© Leah Crain

Make Your Own Dressmaker's Dummy With Duct Tape
You saw it on the Web first. **Leanna's Duct Tape Double Studio (http://www. leanna.com/DuctTapeDouble)** offers instructions for making a dressmaker's form with tape. You can't make it alone—you'll need to invite a friend over, one you won't feel embarrassed standing in front of semi-nude and covered with tape. You'll also find directions on making a dressmaker's form with plastic wrap and plaster at **Rina's Sewing Home Page (http://www.gl.umbc.edu/~rabzug1/sewing/plaster.html)**.

 Help Sewing for People with Special Needs

E very so often someone writes us asking if we can point them to help on the Web for sewing for those with special physical needs. We've scoured the Web and haven't been able to come up with a lot of Web sites that offer this kind of specialized sewing help. However, there are a few good places to look. Head first to the **Disabilities Forum at About.Com** (**http://disabilities.about.com**). The forum offers an extensive up-to-date directory to companies all over the Net that sell clothing—as well as clothing patterns for those with special needs. Many of these companies have online catalogs.

You should also head to the many cyberspace support groups for specific physical conditions. Many of these groups offer clothing hints and advice. For instance, we've listed in this chapter a link to the International MS Support Foundation, which offers a free pattern for sewing a vest with ice packs in it for those who can't risk becoming overheated. To find support groups head to one of the big Web searchers—our favorite is **Excite** (**http://www.excite.com**)—and simply type the name of the disability or condition.

DRESSING WITH PRIDE
http://members.aol.com/sewtique/pride.htm

You can order books on how to modify store-bought clothing and how to create your own solutions to dressing problems from this non-profit group that provides assistance to the elderly and disabled.

"MAKE YOUR OWN COOL VEST" BY JAN THIEME
http://aspin.asu.edu/msnews/vest.htm

The International MS Support Foundation offers directions for sewing a vest with pockets for ice packs.

MAKE IT EASY: SMALL WHEELCHAIR TOTE BAG
http://members.xoom.com/make_it_easy/wheel.html

 Patterns from the Home Sewing Association Web Site

"SUZY BAGS" FOR MASTECTOMY PATIENTS
http://www.sewing.org/careshare/suzybags.html

HOSPITAL BED SADDLEBAG
http://www.sewing.org/careshare/saddlebag.html

WALKER CADDY
http://www.sewing.org/careshare/walker.html

LAP ROBE FOR WHEELCHAIR USERS
http://www.sewing.org/careshare/laprobe.html

IOWA STATE UNIVERSITY SPECIAL NEEDS CLOTHING ADVICE
http://www.exnet.iastate.edu/Pages/pubs/cl.htm

*You'll find several articles on selecting and sewing clothing for special needs in the university's publication archive. The articles offer tailoring and design suggestions for both comfort and giving a good impression. You need the free **Adobe Acrobat** browser plugin (**http://www.adobe.com**) to read the articles.*

"OLDER PEOPLE: WHERE SHOULD THEY GO FOR CLOTHES?" BY ROSE MARIE TONDL
http://www.ianr.unl.edu/PUBS/nebfacts/nf83.htm

This article from the University of Nebraska Extension explores clothing modifications and choices for the elderly as well as the handicapped, such as shoulder openings for T-shirts. It offers a directory of firms that sell specialized clothing.

WEARABLES
http://www.blvd.com/wearables/index.html

Here's a pattern for men's pants designed for easy dressing.

"POST-OPERATIVE CLOTHING: PLAN AHEAD FOR COMFORT DURING RECOVERY" FROM OHIO STATE UNIVERSITY
http://www.ag.ohio-state.edu/~ohioline/hyg-fact/5000/5502.html

This wonderful article by Joyce Smith and Norma Pitts tells you what kind of clothing you'll need to feel comfortable after different kinds of surgery. It covers everything from undergarments to hosiery and nightwear. They discuss garment cuts and offer lots of tips to help one who is incapacitated feel better about themselves.

TIP

Use 3M's Scotchlite Reflective Fabric to Help Make a Wheelchair User or the Visually Impaired More Visible to Traffic
Face it, drivers often don't look when they're zooming through intersections. They don't see the red flag bobbing at the top of a wheelchair. They don't see the red and white cane of a blind pedestrian. Visit **3M's** Web site (**http://www.mmm.com/scotchlite/info.html**) to learn about a new highly reflective fabric that will make you or your loved one more visible to cars.

CHAPTER 16

Help Sewing with Kids—and for Kids

What's more fun than an afternoon spent sewing some kid-cuddly toy or jumpsuit? An afternoon spent sewing with kids! Kids will teach you the silliest things about sewing. Why sew a seam when you can staple it? Haute couture always looks better with stickers. And there is no sewing mistake that can't be fixed by gluing glitter over it. Here are some Web sites that will fill you with ideas for sewing projects to tackle with the scout troop—plus a few that offer help for sewing clothes for kids.

Free Help Sewing for Kids

SEW4KIDS4FUN

(**http://www.quiltropolis.com/NewMailinglists.asp**) is a mailing list discussion group run through Quiltropolis. Members share tips and pattern recommendations for sewing for kids. The list is for those who sew for kids "just for fun"—in contrast to the other Quiltropolis mailing list **ChildSew** (see Chapter 22) which is populated by those who sew for children commercially.

"SEWING FOR CHILDREN" BY ROSE MARIE TONDL

http://www.ianr.unl.edu/PUBS/textiles/heg137.htm

*Tondl tells you all you need to know about fitting, measuring, and sewing children's clothes in this cyber-pamphlet from the University of Nebraska Extension. Head the extension's main archive site (**http://www.ianr.unl.edu/PUBS/textiles**) to see other related articles.*

USENET NEWSGROUP TEXTILE FAQ
ftp://rtfm.mit.edu/pub/usenet/news.answers/crafts/textiles/faq/part2

The second part of the frequently asked question file assembled from messages posted in the Usenet textile crafts newsgroup includes postings on sewing for kids.

Sew 3M Scotchlite Reflective Material to Your Child's Clothes
Make your child more visible to traffic by sewing 3M's new Scotchlite Reflective fabric onto their clothes. It's similar to the reflective stickers and tape you can buy in sewing stores, except that it's not brittle and doesn't crumble. It's also available by the yard. You can sew it into garments, or use it to sew panels on garments. Read more about this revolutionary fabric at the Web site of **3M** (**http://www.mmm.com/scotchlite**).

Moms have special sewing needs, too, especially when they're nursing. One excellent resource is **The Nursing Moms Sewing Mailing List Discussion Group** (**http://www.kjsl.com/~momto3/nmsl/list.html**). They discuss issues related to sewing for nursing moms, especially converting ready-to-wear patterns for nursing access. The group also relies on commercial patterns from **Elizabeth Lee Designs** (**http://www.elizabethlee.com/index.htm**).

Free Help Sewing With Kids

ABOUT.COM'S SUMMER SEWING WITH THE KIDS
http://sewing.about.com/library/blsumer.htm

HOME SEWING ASSOCIATION KIDS PAGE
http://www.sewing.org/kidspage/index.html

SEW YOUNG, SEW FUN FOR TEENS
http://www.sewyoungsewfun.com

Sewing-machine maker Husqvarna Viking offers directions for lots of very creative projects including a locker organizer and handbags.

QUILTING WITH CHILDREN
http://www.thecraftstudio.com/qwc

Heddi Craft, an elementary school teacher, describes quilting projects she has organized with kids.

HANDS ON CRAFTS FOR KIDS
http://www.craftsforkids.com

This Web site is based on the TV show of the same name, and includes a project page that is updated regularly.

SEWING PROSE FOR KIDS & PARENTS
http://www.sewingprose.com/resources.html

4H CLOTHING PROJECT REFERENCE MANUAL FROM MISSISSIPPI STATE UNIVERSITY
http://www.ext.msstate.edu:80/pubs/pub1302.htm

This primer from the Mississippi State University Extension fills 4Hers in on sewing tools, measuring, marking, the basics of hand sewing, clothing repair, the parts of a sewing machine, and more.

SEWGEEKY...
CREATIVITY GONE TERRIBLY WRONG
http://www.sewgeeky.com/index1.html

You won't find any sewing projects per say on this site, but teenagers will love "SewGeeky's" colorfully written ramblings about growing up creative and trying to find her niche in the adult world. Your teen will especially relate to her description of what happened when she went a little nuts trying to transform her bedroom with stencils (we did). SewGeeky's first love is sewing and you'll read about that too.

Why Not Get the Kids Sewing to Help Others?
Click the "Stitches That Serve" icon on Viking's teen sewing Web site **Sew Young, Sew Fun** (**http://www.sewyoungsewfun.com**) for information on teen sewing charity projects. Projects like "comfort caps" for childhood cancer patients or "cozy coats" for needy kids.

free Stuff for Doll and Teddy Bear Makers

For years the dolls and bears Judy sewed were sorry looking confections with buttons for eyes. Sure, she still talked to them, and sometimes they talked back. But then she found other dollmakers on the Web. Her life changed. Completely. Forever. Soon she was bewigging dolls with neon-colored wool, painting their faces with glitter paint, and palavering in Internet chat rooms about how to tailor poodle skirts for Chatty Cathys. Join in the dollmaking fun on the Internet and your life, too, will never be the same.

Big Web Sites for Dollmakers

These are the hot spots for dollmakers on the Web. If you're looking for hard-to-find dollmaking supplies or answers to questions about dollmaking—or you're just looking for other dollmakers to talk to, these are the places to go.

DOLL STREET AT DOLLTROPOLIS
http://www.dolltropolis.com/dollstreet

Molly Finnegan's clever and witty site serves as cyber depot to doll-makers who just want to have fun making dolls. You'll find the Doll Street Dreams Doll Club, the Chatterer's Cafe & Carwash, the Doll Street Gazette, and much more. They have a terrific member page, called **Pearl's URLs,** *with links to the Web sites of dollmakers around the Web (*http://www.dolltropolis.com/dollstreet/pearlsurls.htm*). You'll also find a free copy of the* **Doll Street Jester Pin Pattern** *(*http://www.dolltropolis.com/dollstreet/pinpattern.htm*).*

THE CLOTH DOLL CONNECTION
http://www.clothdollconnection.com
http://www.clothdollconnection.com/FreePatterns.html

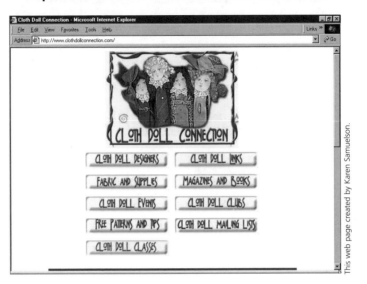

This web page created by Karen Samuelson.

Karen Samuelson's Cloth Doll Connection is a fabulous site where you'll find dollmaking tips, links to free patterns all over the Web, information on mailing lists for dollmakers and dollmaking clubs around the country, lists of fabric suppliers, and also information on contacting famous designers, both online and by mail.

DOLL NET
http://www.thedollnet.com

All dollmaking in cyberspace points toward Doll Net, where you'll find free doll patterns, bulletin boards, chats, a mailing list, a gallery of dolls crafted by other cyber dollmakers, and much more.

CLOTHART FROM MARTY DONNELLAN
http://www.martydoll.com/index.html.

Marty Donnellan's Web site offers tips and techniques, a mailing list for doll artists, a gallery of dolls, and some hard-to-find supplies for doll makers.

MIMI'S DOLLMAKER'S PARADISE
http://www.mimidolls.com

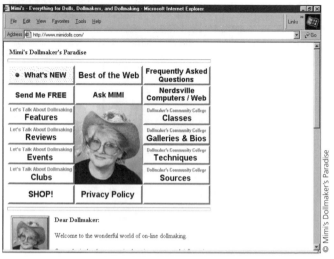

Jim and Gloria J. "Mimi" Winer run this marvelous site which includes lots of doll photos, gossip on the professional world of dollmaking, and links to all the good doll crafting stuff on the Web. Plus you'll find Mimi's dollmaker's handbook, which is a treasure trove of good advice and direction.

 DELPHI'S ARTIST DOLL FORUM
http://www0.delphi.com/artdolls

 **Travel the Doll Ring
to Meet Other Doll Lovers**
Like to surf the Web sites of other doll lovers? Head to the **Doll Ring (http://members.tripod.com/~hollie/dollring.html)**. If you want sites devoted to cloth dolls, head to the links page at the **Cloth Doll Connection (http://www.clothdollconnection.com/ClothDollLinks.html)**. You don't need to join the ring in order to visit the sites.

Web Sites of Dollmaking Magazines

THE CLOTH DOLL MAGAZINE
http://www.theclothdoll.com/index.html

 DOLLMAKING & DOLL ARTISAN
http://www.DollmakingArtisan.com

Doll Artisan *is a magazine devoted to making porcelain dolls.*
Dollmaking *is for makers of porcelain and sculpted dolls. You'll find a message board for dollmakers on this site—and sometimes you can snare a trial issue of one of the magazines.*

 More Free Doll Patterns

"MEGAN" DOLL PATTERN BY KAREN CUSICK
http://www.theclothdoll.com/megan.html

Karen offers illustrated instructions for sewing a 9" jointed doll with hair and a painted face. She also offers clothing patterns.

"COUSIN EZRA" FROM FAIRFIELD
http://www.poly-fil.com/crafts/CraftProject.html

Make a giant snail out of knits. This is a pattern the kids will enjoy, from poly-stuffing maker Fairfield.

CRAFTY VISIONS NEWSLETTER PATTERNS
http://wwvisions.com/newsletter

JOINTED BALLERINA BUNNY PATTERN FROM GAIL KELLISON
http://www.netins.net/showcase/dollpatterns/Freepattern2.htm

JUDI'S DOLLS
http://www.thedollnet.com/judi/index.html

THE SWEATER GIRL FROM CASEY DOLLS
http://www.caseydolls.com/sweater.html

Dollmaker Jacqueline Casey offers directions for making an appealing doll out of an old sweater.

CHERUB PATTERN FROM GAIL'S STITCH N' SPLINTER PATTERNS
http://www.thedollnet.com/stitchnsplinter/index.html

DRACO THE DRAGON PIN FROM LEE MENCONI STEIGER
http://members.tripod.com/~wingsnthings/draco.com/

HOW TO MAKE AN <EXPLETIVE DELETED> DOLL
http://www.huskins.com/strega/dammit.html

Do you sometimes fantasize about being seven years old again and whacking your doll against the wall in frustration? Weezie's Warped World offers a pattern for a doll that you can beat the stuffing out of without feeling any remorse. She also offers an accompanying poem. Check our her recipes for cooking with 7Up and "growing a brain."

More Free Dollmaking How-Tos

MIMI'S HANDBOOK FOR DOLLMAKERS
http://www.mimidolls.com/handbook/handbook.htm

*Gloria J. "Mimi" Winer offers this amazing resource which offers
advice on just about every subject of importance to dollmakers.*

NOT JUST DOLLS GAZETTE
http://notjustdollmakers.com/gazette.html

ANTONETTE CELY'S DOLLMAKING HELP
http://www.cely.com/doll.html

*This world-renowned doll artist offers illustrated tips and tutorials
on a variety of techniques including how to properly fashion hands.*

 **LOOKING FOR A DOLL CLUB IN YOUR TOWN?**
The Bluebonnet Craft Network
(**http://bluebonnetvillage.com/dolls-1.htm**) offers an up-to-
date and comprehensive list of clubs for dollmakers around
the country.

 Free Dollmaking Discussions

The Internet plays host to many wonderful discussion groups
for dollmakers. Amazingly, all these groups are very different.
Some are for professional or aspiring doll artists, others are for
crafters who sew dolls not only but also other stuffed creatures
like Teddy bears; some are serious-minded and require that par-
ticipants stick to designated topics, while other groups are laid-
back and encourage chit-chat about spouses and children.
Before you sign up, read the rules of the list carefully.

You'll find an excellent up-to-date list of dollmakers' discussion groups at **The Cloth Doll Connection's Mailing List** (**http://www.clothdollconnection.com/EventsandList.html#CLASSES**), and lots of the big sites listed above also host discussion groups.

BLACK CLOTH DOLL ART
http://www.onelist.com/subscribe.cgi/blackclothdollart

This group discusses crafting dolls with ethnic skin fabrics.

CLOTH DOLLMAKER
http://www.onelist.com/subscribe.cgi/Cloth_Dollmaker

DOLLIES DOWN UNDER DIGEST
http://members.xoom.com/dolliesunder/join.html

Two Aussie dollmakers started this list, but you don't have to be from the Land of the Koala to join.

DOLLS N' SUCH SISTERHOOD

Pat Van Horn (vanhorn@servtech.com) runs this amicable list for makers of dolls, teddies, and other stuffed animals.

DOLLMAKERS
http://www.everink.com

Dollmakers is for professional and beginning dollmakers who want to talk shop. Pointless chit-chat is discouraged.

FRIENDS OF THE CLOTH DOLL
http://www.dollnet.com/clothdolls/subscribe.html

This discussion group is for anyone who loves cloth dolls, from artists to collectors and retailers. Discussions stick to the topic, but the group is lively.

NOT JUST DOLLMAKERS
http://notjustdollmakers.com

This chatty group is comprised of people who make dolls, but also do other things—like hold day jobs—and just want to be friends.

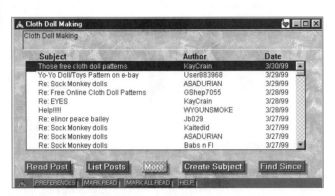

Join Other Doll & Bear Makers on AOL & Compuserve

If you're a member of America Online you can chat with other dollmakers in the Crafts & Needlework Forum. Use the keyword **sewing**. In the pop-up sewing menu scroll down to the Sewing Board. You'll need to scroll through the message list to find the dollmaking discussions. You'll also find a small library of dollmaking patterns and pictures in the Crafts Community library. Use the keyword **sewing**, then scroll down to Crafts Community and click.

If you're a member of Compuserve, use the go word **sewing** to get to the Sewing & Quilting Forum. Scroll to the Dolls & Bears category. Click on Messages to chat with other doll and bear makers. Click Files to access a file library that includes a few free patterns, some bear-making tips, supplier lists, and more.

SURF THE WEB SITES OF
DOLL ARTISTS FOR GREAT PATTERNS

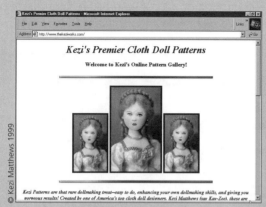

© Kezi Matthews 1999

*Doll artists like Kezi Matthews (**http://www.thekeziworks.com**) offer galleries of doll patterns you can view and buy on their Web sites.*

There are many, many, *many* doll artists who sell patterns from their Web sites. In most cases these aren't the ragdoll patterns you'll find in Kansas. You'll find patterns for everything from wood nymphs to car mechanics, and a million exotic beauties in between. And chances are that you won't find them in any stores. We can't encourage you enough: surf the sites of dollmakers, look at the patterns they offer for sale, and try a few, even if they look difficult. You'll be surprised at the talent that may be hidden within your hands. The two best places to start your journey are:

DOLL NET
http://www.thedollnet.com

KAREN SAMUELSON'S LIST OF CLOTH DOLL PATTERN MAKERS AT CLOTH DOLL CONNECTION
http://www.clothdollconnection.com/ClothDollDesigners.html

Want a catalog from elinor peace bailey? How about "Annette the Lizard Lady?" Karen offers a clickable directory of dozens of doll artists.

Big Web Sites for Teddy Bear Makers

Head to these Web sites to find inspiration, assistance, and fun.

 ## TEDDY BEARS ON THE NET
http://www.tbonnet.com/second_index.html

Terry Bauman maintains this marvelous site full of book reviews, links to suppliers, Teddy magazines, museums, and discussion groups. You can buy Teddy bear making kits, read Teddy design hints, and have a Teddy tell your fortune.

BEARWORLD!
http://www.bearworld.com

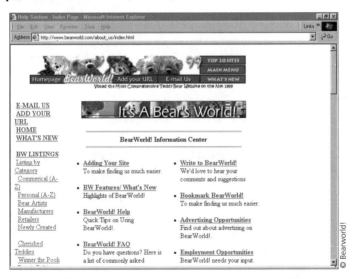

BearWorld! offers the biggest selection of Teddy bear links on the Net. You'll also find technical advice and a directory of artists who sell custom-made bears on the Web—great sites for inspiration.

BEARLY HEAVEN
http://bluebonnetvillage.com/bheaven.htm

🛒 SPARE BEAR PARTS
http://www.SpareBear.com

This retailer of bear-making goodies offers a huge database of tips and how-tos on everything ranging from joint installation, furs, repairs, how to make a new bear look old and vice versa, needle sculpting, and installing music box keys. They also offer a free newsletter.

 Free Teddy Bear Patterns

THE TEDDY BEAR TIMES PATTERN ARCHIVE
http://www.teddybeartimes.com/patterns/listing.htm

This British magazine for lovers and makers of Teddy bears offers free downloadable patterns for bears, clothes, and accessories.

Take a DollMaking Class In Cyberspace

Do you live miles from a craft store that offers dollmaking classes? Why not take a class on the Web? A growing number of Web sites offer "classes" in cyberspace where you can learn how to paint faces, draft doll clothing patterns, and form perfect hands. They usually cost from $25 to $35, not including supplies. Once you pay the fee you can tap into a password-protected bulletin board or Web site where you'll converse with the other class members and teachers. You'll receive an illustrated pattern and instructions. You'll need to provide your own materials, but can often buy them from the Web site or from recommended Web retailers. The following Web sites offer classes in dollmaking:

CLOTHART WORKSHOPS
http://www.martydoll.com/Workshops.htm

CRAFTY COLLEGE
http://craftycollege.com/academics/index.html

DOLLTROPOLIS CLASSES ONLINE
http://www.dolltropolis.com/dollstreet/unisignup.htm

Surf the Cloth Doll Maker's Web Ring!
Visit the Web sites of other doll makers by surfing this Web ring. Head to the links page at the **Cloth Doll Connection** (**http://www.clothdollconnection.com/ClothDollLinks.html**). You don't need to join the ring in order to visit the sites.

Find Hard-to-Find Doll Making Supplies at The Doll Makers Suppliers List from the **Doll Makers Discussion Group** (**http://www.wtco.net/homepages/cocuzzo/suppliers.html**)

Free Teddy Bear Making Discussions

TEDDY BEARS MAILING LIST
http://www.cybear.austin.com

This group talks about just about everything relating to Teddy bears, including collecting, crafting, restoring, and enjoying them.

DOLL NET'S TEDDY BEAR BULLETIN BOARD
http://www.wwvisions.com/craftbb/teddy.html

BEARWORLD CHAT ROOMS & BULLETIN BOARD
http://www.bearworld.com

BEAR ARTISTS ONLINE
http://bearartists.com

*In order to join this group you must be a commercial bear artist with a Web site where you sell your bears. Members link to each other via a Web ring, and enjoy an ICQ user's group—which is a chat room using the chat software from Mirabilis (*http://www.icq.com*).*

Free Help for Doll and Bear Makers Who Sew for Those in Need

THE "DOLLY HUGS" PATTERN
http://www.cely.com/dollyhugs.html

"Dolly hugs" is the sign-off many dollmakers use at the end of their e-mail messages, and it inspired doll artist Antonette Cely to design these special patterns for children in crisis. The bear or doll "hugs" the child by wrapping its arms around the child's neck so its face presses against the child's cheek.

"BEAR HUGS" PATTERN
http://www.cely.com/bearhugs.html

GOOD BEARS OF THE WORLD
http://www.goodbearsoftheworld.org

Maybe your local police or fire department already hands out
Teddy bears to children facing trauma. If not, why not start a club
to help them do it? Several organizations exist solely to dispense
Teddy bears to children in need. Why not visit them to get help to
start your own Teddy "grassroots movement?"

TEDDY CARE
http://www.teddycare.com

HOME SEWING ASSOCIATION
"EMERGENCY BEAR" PATTERN
http://www.sewing.org/careshare/stuffdolls.html
http://www.sewing.org/careshare/teddybear.html

The HSA offers a simple stuffed bear pattern for a toy that emergency medical technicians can keep on hand in an ambulance.

🛒 Supplies for Doll and Teddy Bear Makers

We often hear from doll and teddy bear makers looking for supplies or patterns that they've been unable to find in local stores or mail-order catalogs. For example: fabrics in ethnic skin colors and the specialized fabric paints that doll artists use—and may even specify by brand—in their patterns. Can they find these things for sale on the Web? they ask. Of course!

The best way to find a supplier for that obscure fabric paint, extra-soft plush, or purple doll wig is to join one of the mailing lists in the previous section and ask for recommendations. Please keep in mind that there are hundreds of retailers on the Web who sell these supplies. We couldn't include them all, but this wee sampling should get you started shopping.

THE DOLLMAKERS SUPPLIERS LIST FROM THE DOLLMAKERS DISCUSSION GROUP
http://www.wtco.net/homepages/cocuzzo/suppliers.html

CLOTHART
http://www.martydoll.com

You'll find fiber paints, pigments, embellishment fibers, and turning tools, as well as patterns from Tonya Boylan, Marty Donnellan, Susanna Oroyan, and Christine Shively at ClothArt.

SISTERS & DAUGHTERS
http://www.sistersanddaughters.com

You'll find face-painting stencils, paints, "pieces and parts" (like fairy wings), an online catalog of doll patterns from well-known (but sometimes hard-to-find) designers.

MONIQUE TRADING CORP.
http://www.monique.com

Monique sells eyes, shoes, wigs, hosiery, and other miniature accessories.

JEAN & KEN NORDQUIST'S COLLECTIBLE DOLL CO.
http://www.jeannordquistdolls.com

The Collectible Doll sells supplies for porcelain dollmakers, including paints, wigs, molds, eyes, and more.

SEWSWEET DOLLS
http://www.caroleecreations.com

This is the home of Carolee and the patterns and kits for those adorable baby dolls with the soft-sculpted faces. Their catalog offers a huge selection of hard-to-find dollmaking tools and supplies like hair looms and eyes.

 **Help for Heirloom and Bridal Sewing**

Heirloom sewing is the sewing of garments that are destined to become family heirlooms, pieces made of fine fabrics like linen, often with the sorts of machine embellishments that prior generations meticulously stitched by hand, like smocking, pin tucks, lace insertions, and embroidery. It's just the kind of thing we love to do in style for weddings, and it's such fun. Veils! Bustles! Delicate, lace-trimmed hankies! But even an experienced seamstress may find the prospect of hemming that satin gown with the six-foot lace train daunting, or fitting that bustle to the back of the dress. You'll find lots of great sewing advice on these Web sites for brides and their seamstresses, as well as some indispensable sites for all manner of heirloom projects.

 Bridal Sewing Web Sites

SEW BRIDAL BY ALICYN EXCLUSIVES
http://www.sewbridal.com

SEW BRIDAL: FABRIC AND LACE DEFINITIONS
http://www.sewbridal.com/html/body_terms.html

Alicyn designs luscious wedding gown patterns for McCall's. She offers special sewing tips and help for each of her McCall's patterns, plus other insights on the whole process. You need to go to your fabric store to buy the patterns, but this Web site should still be your first stop in shopping for bridal gown patterns.

BRIDAL FABRIC AND LACE CHOICES
http://members.aol.com/KALDesign/fabric.html

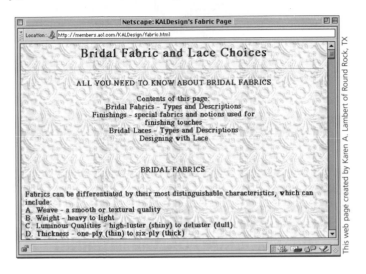

Netscape: KALDesign's Fabric Page

Location: http://members.aol.com/KALDesign/fabric.html

Bridal Fabric and Lace Choices

ALL YOU NEED TO KNOW ABOUT BRIDAL FABRICS

Contents of this page:
Bridal Fabrics – Types and Descriptions
Finishings – special fabrics and notions used for finishing touches
Bridal Laces – Types and Descriptions
Designing with Lace

BRIDAL FABRICS

Fabrics can be differentiated by their most distinguishable characteristics, which can include:
A. Weave – a smooth or textural quality
B. Weight – heavy to light
C. Luminous Qualities – high-luster (shiny) to deluster (dull)
D. Thickness – one-ply (thin) to six-ply (thick)

This web page created by Karen A. Lambert of Round Rock, TX

COUTURE TECHNIQUES FOR BRIDAL
http://members.aol.com/KALDesign/couture.html

CHOOSING READY TO WEAR
VERSUS CUSTOM MADE
http://members.aol.com/KALDesign/info.html

Karen A. Lambert offers several excellent articles on couture techniques and choosing fabrics and laces.

"WEDDING GOWN FITTING TIPS"
BY PEGGY BENDEL IN SEW NEWS
http://www.sewnews.com/library/tips4.htm

"BONING FOR COSTUME, EVENING,
AND BRIDAL WEAR" BY LINDA SPARKS
http://www.fabrics.net/boning.htm

Free Help with Smocking

Many heirloom sewing projects involve smocking, either by hand or on the machine. It's an old-fashioned art, but the Internet is a wonderful resource for stitchers who want to pursue it.

THE SMOCKING CONNECTION
http://www.interlog.com/~gouldhop/smocking.html

You'll find beginner's smocking directions on choosing and preparing fabric, selecting thread, and gathering pleats.

"SMOCKING ON THE SEWING MACHINE" FROM ELNA
http://www.elnausa.com/projects/98dec/dec98.htm

CREATIVE SMOCKING ON THE INTERNET
http://www.smocking.com

This site is geared for retailers who carry smocking supplies—it has information on the newest stuff, and what's upcoming in smocking magazines. But if you can't find smocking supplies in your neighborhood this site will lead you to retailers who can help.

THE SMOCKING ARTS GUILD OF AMERICA
http://www.smocking.org

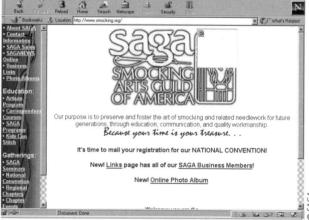

© SAGA

Free Sewing Project How-Tos

WEDDING PROJECT DIRECTIONS FROM THE HOME SEWING ASSOCIATION

- **Romantic Ring Pillow by Lucinda Ganderton**
  http://www.sewing.org/project/ringpillow.html

- **Satin Wedding Purse by Sew Easy Textiles**
  http://www.sewing.org/project/purse.html

OFFRAY RIBBON'S WEDDING COLLECTION
http://www.offray.com/117.html

HEIRLOOM BABY BONNET AND WEDDING HANDKERCHIEF PATTERN BY ADELINE BRILL
http://www.eel.ufl.edu/~ineluki/hanky.html

 Heirloom Sewing Discussion Groups

Quiltropolis (http://www.quiltropolis.com/NewMailinglists.asp) runs a mailing list discussion group for heirloom sewing fans. Topics range from French hand sewing to lace shaping, sewing with silk ribbon and using pleaters.

You'll also find a discussion group at **Delphi's Heirloom Sewing & Smocking Forum (http://www0.delphi.com/heirloom)**.

Finally, if you're just getting started, tap into **Lydia's Heirloom Sewing Center (http://www.lydias.com/qheirbasics.html)** to read a glossary of heirloom stitching terms, plus advice on fabric, stabilizers, and thread.

Looking for Hard-to-Find Laces, Ribbons, and Other Supplies?

There are many Web sites that sell some of the more esoteric heirloom stitching supplies, such as English and Swiss laces; ribbons for use in Edwardian-style millinery; and fluttery, fine linens. Some of our favorite sites: **Victoria Louise, Mercers (http://www.fred.net/stull/victoria.html)** and **Garden Fairies Heirloom and Special Fabrics (http://members.aol.com/ garfairies/heir.html)**. Searching for a special antique lace to trim that dress, veil, or handkerchief? Head to the Web site of **Lacis (http://www.lacis.com)**, a Berkeley, California lace and stitching store (3163 Adeline St., Berkeley, CA 94703, 510/843-7178) that will help you find just about anything lace-related, whether it's new or vintage. They offer a bridal service. Describe your dress pattern and the sort of lace you're looking for, and they'll hunt their extensive resources from around the world. Then they'll send you photocopies of their choices. Plus, web auctions like **eBay (http://www.ebay.com)** are great spots to hunt for vintage and modern bridal gown patterns—and other used vintage and modern bridal accessories like headpieces, gloves, veils, cake tops, and more.

More Bridal Web Sites

These sites don't offer sewing help, but they offer advice on every other aspect of planning a wedding.

BRIDAL GOWNS.COM
http://www.BridalGowns.com

WEDDINGS411.COM
http://www.wedding411.com

THE ULTIMATE INTERNET WEDDING GUIDE
http://www.ultimatewedding.com

WEDDING IDEAS
http://www.weddingideas.com

WEDDING TIPS ONLINE
http://www.weddingtips.com

A GUIDE TO MUSIC FOR YOUR WEDDING FROM THE MUSIC LIBRARY AT THE UNIVERSITY OF VIRGINIA
http://www.lib.virginia.edu/MusicLib/collect/wedding.html

BRIDAL SHOWER GAMES, IDEAS, AND THEMES BY KATHEE KELLY
http://www.imagebydesign.com/kathee/bridal/

 **Fabric Embellishment How-Tos**

Maybe you're never satisfied sewing a vest or skirt and leaving it at that. Like a blank canvas, the garment calls to you for embellishment; you need to beribbon it, bead it, embroider on it, and bedazzle it. If you feel that no garment should be left blank, you'll find lots of help on the Web—from tutorials on pin-tucking to fabric-painting or velvet embossing and gluing sequins on fabric. All the major sewing Web sites we talk about in Chapter 2 offer embellishment help and ideas. You'll also find lots of embellishment chat in the sewing forums of America Online and Compuserve. Check out all these Web sites and your wearables will indeed become wearable art.

ABOUT.COM'S SEWING & FABRIC EMBELLISHMENT FROM DEBBIE COLGROVE
http://sewing.about.com/library/weekly/aa052298.htm

DYED & GONE TO HEAVEN BY CARON
http://caron-net.com

LESLIE LEVISON'S "CRAZY QUILT PATCHWORK BLOCK" ONLINE CLASS
http://www.caron-net.com/classes/classmayfiles/clasmay1.html

NANCY ZIEMAN'S CRAZY PIECING WITH DECORATIVE STITCHING
http://www.nancysnotions.com/SewingRoomLibrary/CrazyPiecing.html

OFFRAY RIBBON
http://www.offray.com/prod.html

Offray offers advice on ribbon care, plus lots of how-tos on making bows, ribbon flowers, and other things to jazz up your projects.

MACHINE APPLIQUÉ, SATIN STITCHING FROM DAVID SMALL
http://small-expressions.com/instruct/text14.htm

WONDERFUL STITCHES
http://www.needlework.com/html/home.html

Wonderful Stitches offers decorative patterns and designs for all types of needlework—and many ideas for embellishing garments and quilts with hand-stitched embroidery.

MAKING GATHERS FROM DELPHI NEEDLEARTS' TIPS & TECHNIQUES
http://www0.delphi.com/needle/tips.html

PURRFECTION ARTISTIC WEARABLES' PERFECTLY FREE PROJECTS
http://www.purrfection.com

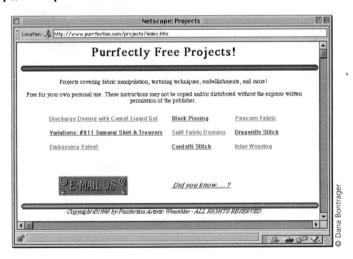

BEADNET
http://www.mcs.net/~simone/beadnet.html

BEADWORK FROM SUZANNE COOPER
http://www.suzannecooper.com/beadmain.html

BEAD TALK
http://www.quiltropolis.com/NewMailinglists.asp

Quiltropolis (**www.quiltropolis.com**) *and Cindy's Crafts run a laid-back discussion group relating to beading and anything bead-related.*

B. SMITH WITH STYLE: VELVET EMBOSSING
http://www.bsmithwithstyle.com/living/air_020798/velvet.html

GLENDA SCOTT'S FABRIC ORIGAMI
http://www.owt.com/gdscott

Why not turn those fabric scraps into ornaments, boxes, and note-card embellishements with Glenda's guidance?

WILDLY WONDERFUL WEARABLES
http://www.wwwearables.com/techniques/index.htm

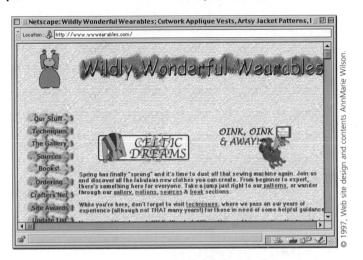

You'll find tips and technique how-tos at this clever site.

HOW-TOS FROM CNT PATTERN CO.

- **How to Pucker Fabric**
  http://www.cntpattern.com/Win/3_SewTips/Puckering.html

- **Double-Needle Tucking Fabric**
  http://www.cntpattern.com/Win/3_SewTips/DoubleNeedle.html

- **Shearing Fabric**
  http://www.cntpattern.com/Win/3_SewTips/Shearing.html

- **Patching Cozy Quilt Fabric**
  http://www.cntpattern.com/Win/3_SewTips/Patching.html

Dye It and Paint It!

There are lots of other things you can do with fabric besides stitch it. You can tie-dye it, batik it, marble it, paint it, stamp it, and stencil it. Companies that sell fabric paint, dye, and other fabric embellishment products offer on their Web sites lots of advice, how-tos, and answers to common questions about using their products.

DHARMA TRADING CO.
http://www.dharmatrading.com

Dharma offers lots of free instruction, like dye painting, discharge paste instructions, and more.

JACQUARD PRODUCTS
http://www.jacquardproducts.com

By the way, Jacquard sells an innovative kit for creating quilts and other items by printing on the fabric in your inkjet printer (http://www.jacquardproducts.com/productpages/kits/ inkjetquiltkit.htm).

PRO CHEMICAL AND DYE, INC.
http://www.prochemical.com

You'll find instructions on how to create the popular suede look when dyeing fabric, creating starburst patterns on silk, and more.

CHAPTER 20

 Help for Drapery Making, Upholstering, And Other Home Dec Projects

Whether your home is an apartment over a busy street or a spacious manse on a hill, nothing transforms it like fabric. Rooms not only look cozier with fabric, but sounds in the rooms sound cozier too. Through your choice of colors and prints you can make a room look larger, or make it seem more intimate. You can in essence make it *yours*. Here are some Web sites that will help you with your big decorating plans.

If you're a professional home decorator (or aspire to be), sign up for the mailing list discussion group **WindowWeb** run by **Quiltropolis (http://www.quiltropolis.com/NewMailinglists.asp)**. There is a modest annual membership fee.

 Free Help for Drapery Making

ABOUT.COM'S CURTAINS AND WINDOW TREATMENTS
http://sewing.about.com/msubcurt.htm

WINDOW TREATMENTS
http://www.golden.net/~leroux/window.htm

Learn how to estimate yardage for pocket top drapery and valances, how to make fast roman shades, and more.

HOW TO MEASURE
YOUR CURTAINS BY LESLIE CURTAINS
http://www.westozweb.com.au/leslies/measure.html

SEAMS TO BE—TAKING MEASUREMENTS
http://www.seamstobe.com/Measuring.htm

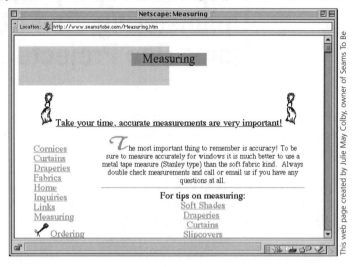

"SEWING VALANCES" FROM JO-ANN FABRICS
http://www.joann.com/project/decorating/quick_valance.html

"SWAG TREATMENTS" FROM JO-ANN FABRICS
http://www.joann.com/project/decorating/swag_treatments.html

DECORATING TIPS AND INNOVATIVE TREATMENT IDEAS FOR WINDOWS
http://www.curtainrods.com/tips.htm

DREAMY ESCAPES FROM
COUNTRY SAMPLER DECORATING IDEAS
http://www.sampler.com/decideas/archivedec98/project2.html

Free Help for Upholstering

UPHOLSTER! MAGAZINE ONLINE
http://www.upholster.com

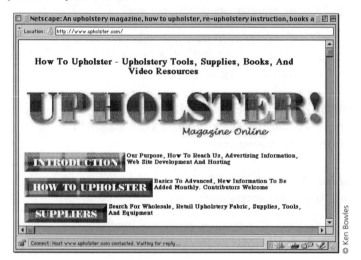

© Ken Bowles

Learn the basics of upholstering and expand your skills with master techniques. You'll find how-tos on installing zippers, using tacking, and how to slipcover an ottoman. You'll even learn how to reupholster your car!

THE FURNITURE WORKS' FURNITURE FACTS: AN UPHOLSTERY PRIMER
http://www.furnitureworks.com/primer.htm

UPHOLSTERY WIZARD
http://www.furnitureworks.com/wizard.htm

A guide to calculating fabric needs for different types of furniture.

HOW TO UPHOLSTER A SLIP SEAT
BY JUDY RICE
http://w3.nai.net/~fabricwk/slipseat.htm

Free Big Home Dec Sewing Web Sites

HOME DECORATING FROM
THE HOME SEWING ASSOCIATION
http://sewing.org/educate/decorating.html

The HSA tells you how to measure beds, windows, and tables for recovering, plus the meanings of fabric terms, how to figure out how much fabric to buy, and more.

HOUSENET'S SEWING IDEAS
http://www.housenet.com/sw/main.asp?CategoryID=5
http://www.housenet.com

WAVERLY FABRICS
http://www.decoratewaverly.com

You'll find lots of decorating ideas and advice for stitching your way to home dec bliss.

Need Cleaning Help?
The folks at **DoItYourself.com** offer help for cleaning and stain removal woes. You'll find advice on cleaning household surfaces like chrome, marble and wrought iron at its their **Cleaning and Housewares Info and FAQs** page (**http://www.doityourself.com/clean**).

Free Home Dec Stitching Projects

COUNTRY SAMPLER MAGAZINE DECORATING PROJECTS
http://www.sampler.com/decideas/decideas.html

A large archive of projects, like window displays, flower arrangements, and a "patchwork cabinet."

BETTER HOMES & GARDENS ONLINE
http://www.bhglive.com/househome/index.html

Head to the "Article Archive" for directions on making lampshades, decorating with sheets, and more.

"HOW TO MAKE A CATHEDRAL WINDOW CUSHION" BY DY TAYLOR
http://www.tower.net.au/~fish/dycraft/cushion/cushion.html

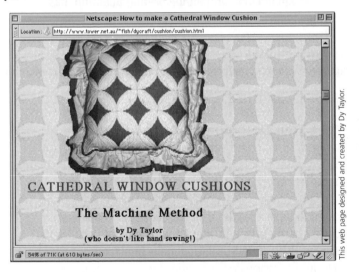

This web page designed and created by Dy Taylor.

Dy Taylor from Perth, Australia explains how to make this pillow entirely by machine.

"HOW TO MAKE SHOWER CURTAINS" FROM HGTV'S *SEW PERFECT*
http://www.hgtv.com/village/villages/crafton/shows/sew/sew_shwrcurtain_intro.html

"STRAIGHT STITCHING A CHAIR SLIP" FROM *THE DETROIT NEWS*
http://detnews.com/homestyl/9602/17/hand/hand.html

FREE HOME DEC STITCHING PROJECTS FROM JO-ANN'S FABRICS

- **Chair Covers**
  http://www.joann.com/project/decorating/chair_cover.html

- **Beautiful Bed Coverings**
  http://www.joann.com/project/decorating/beautiful_bed_coverings.html

- **Tapestry Pillows**
  http://www.joann.com/project/decorating/tapestry_pillows.html

Make Your Decorating Energy Efficient.
Thinking of stitching some window quilts to keep out those winter drafts? And how tightly should you insulate that attic before transforming it into a sewing room? Colorado State University Cooperative Extension offers free downloadable consumer publications on making your house energy efficient (**http://www.colostate.edu/Depts/CoopExt/PUBS/CONSUMER/pubcons.html#energy**). Pamphlets include discussions on insulating, weather stripping doors, using wood stoves, and other topics.

CHAPTER 21

Patterns and Ideas for Sewing Charity Projects

One of the best things about cyberspace is how many needlework-related charity projects are going on wherever you look. Stitchers are a generous bunch, and in just about any e-mail mailing list group you'll find stitchers organizing efforts to sew preemie gowns for hospitals, dolls for abused children, or caps for chemotherapy patients. Here are some Web sites that offer patterns, ideas, and contacts for sewing charity projects.

✋ Head to Chapter 17, Free Stuff for Doll and Teddy Bear Makers, for more links to patterns and charity projects. You'll find links to free patterns for chemotherapy turbans in Chapter 12, Free Help for Sewing Hats and Outerwear.

PROJECT LINUS
http://www.projectlinus.org

Project Linus has delivered over 80,000 home-made security blankets to pediatric cancer patients and other children in trauma through its chapters throughout the United States.

PROJECT WARM FUZZIES
http://users.accessus.net/~davenkim/pwf/intro.html

Project Warm Fuzzies provides quilts to children undergoing treatment at St. Jude's and at Shriners' hospitals.

THE HOME SEWING ASSOCIATION'S CARING & SHARING

http://www.sewing.org/careshare/index.html

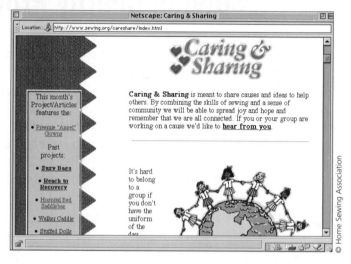

The HSA offers free patterns for chemotherapy turbans, a hospital bed saddlebag, a walker caddy, "Suzy bags" for mastectomy patients, a walker caddy, a lap robe for wheelchair users, preemie "angel" gowns, emergency teddy bears, and more. The HSA also offers advise on organizing group sewing projects, plus Web links and contact information for getting in touch with agencies that need these items.

SEWING WITH NANCY'S SEW A SMILE

http://www.nancysnotions.com/sewsmile.html

Tap into Nancy Zieman's extensive database of sewing charity projects around the country that are stitching up everything from sleeping bags for kids in homeless shelters to hats and scarves for disaster victims.

THE NAMES PROJECT FOUNDATION: AIDS MEMORIAL QUILT

http://www.aidsquilt.org/quilt

NEWBORNS IN NEED
http://www.newbornsinneed.com/

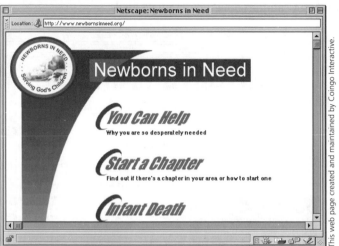

This web page created and maintained by Coingo Interactive.

Newborns In Need stitches clothes and toys for sick and needy newborns in hospitals around the country.

ABC QUILTS PROJECTS
http://www.jbu.edu/ABCQuilts

ABC QUILTS FOR KOSOVO
http://www.jbu.edu/ABCQuilts/Kosovo.htm

ABC is a national volunteer group that provides quilts to HIV-infected and abandoned babies in hospitals around the country.

QUILTS OVER KOSOVO
http://www.globaldevelopment.org/quilts.htm

Learn how you can stitch up quilts for refugee camps. Quilts are actually more practical than blankets for refugees because they can be strung over rope to create temporary shelters.

RAGING LIGHT PROJECT:
THE BREAST CANCER NAMES BANNER
http://www.quiltart.com/judy/ragingl1.html

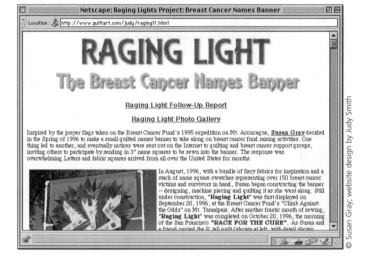

When Susan Gray stitched a small banner quilted with the names of breast cancer victims to take with her on breast cancer fund raising activities, she had no idea how quickly the idea would spread. Read about the project and find out how you can participate.

THE SEWING LIST'S CHARITY SEWING PROJECT
http://www.inil.com/users/jkpage/charity.htm

This Web site was put up by an e-mail discussion group some time ago to share ideas on charity sewing projects. It still includes some great ideas, helpful messages posted by members, and a few patterns too, like **Heartwarmer Coats by Shirley Adams** (**http://www.inil.com/users/jkpage/heart.htm**)—a pattern for a simple Polar Fleece coat that is appreciated by organizations like the Salvation Army.

SOCK BABIES
http://www.deck.com/people/4hsew/index.html

Ethany Nelson shares directions for simple-to-make sock dolls for use in charity projects.

SEWING PROJECTS FOR CRAFT FAIRS & FUND DRIVES, FROM ABOUT.COM
http://sewing.about.com/library/blfund.htm

DOLLS FOR TAMARA
http://members.delphi.com/cheripie/index.html

In memory of her baby girl, Sharon sews dolls and stuffed animals and accepts donations of the same for local hospitals, shelters, and churches for sick and abused children.

Be Skeptical of Mass-Mailed E-Mail Pitches for Sympathy

It happens all the time. Some normally intelligent and skeptical stitcher forwards to all her friends an e-mail chain letter imparting a tale of woe and a plea for money. The message includes a request for recipients to forward it on to 25 other friends. *Most of these messages are hoaxes.* We plead with you: *Delete them.* Also delete any e-mail chain letters that request that you 1) e-mail some government agency to help save the Internet from ill-conceived legislation or save public television from the same; 2) e-mail some company or person because they have promised to donate 1 cent for every e-mail they receive to some charity; 3) e-mail some kid who's supposedly trying to set a world record for receiving more e-mail than anyone else. In other words, *delete any e-mail chain letter you receive!*

While we're on the subject, we often receive e-mail mass-mailings or "spams" from people who are supposedly collecting quilts for some charity we've never heard of. Be skeptical of these too. Check out the charity—and the individual too—before mailing off any donation.

CHAPTER 22

free Help for Sewing Entrepreneurs

Wouldn't it be lovely to earn a living by stitching the things you love? The reality is that running a sewing business requires one to devote considerable time to nasty tasks like collecting on unpaid invoices, dealing with difficult customers, and appeasing the IRS. Networking with other sewers who run home businesses can be your ticket to success (and sanity). The **Sew Pros Network** (**http://www.sewstorm.com/sewpros.htm**) run by Karen Maslowski, author of *How to Start Making Money with Your Sewing*, is an e-mail discussion group of sewers who run small businesses.

The **SewBiz** mailing list group, run by Evalena Heinrich and Colleen Jones through **Quiltropolis** (**http://www.quiltropolis.com/ NewMailinglists.asp**), is another good list to join. **ChildSew** is a mailing list for sewers who sew children's clothing professionally, whether part-time, at home, or at a large company. It's run by Robin Culbertson and Eileen Lloyd and is also available through Quiltropolis. **Professional Crafters** (**http://www.freeyellow.com/ members4/prof-craft**) is a discussion group for not only sewers, but also other types of crafters with businesses.

If you subscribe to **America Online** head to Janet Attard's craft business forum by typing **CraftBiz** in the keyword box. Or, visit her on the Web at **Business Know-How.Com** (**http://www.businessknowhow.com**).

The Usenet newsgroup **alt.crafts.professional** is devoted to discussing the problems of running a crafts business, but you'll find that the above mailing lists are a better resource.

Big Sewing Business Web Sites

SEW STORM PUBLISHING
http://www.sewstorm.com/biztips.htm

Netscape: Biz Tips

Location: http://www.sewstorm.com/biztips.htm

SewStorm Publishing

Books, articles and other support materials for anyone in the sewing professions.

Business Tips

Every month we will have a new article on business, as it pertains to sewing.

This month's article is on marketing for sewing professionals, especially those in the custom clothing business.

Face to Face Marketing

⊕ SewStorm Publishing 1999

Also Read these Past Articles:

Part I of Health Insurance

Part II of Health Insurance

Karen Maslowski offers excellent advice on topics like obtaining health insurance, plus links to Web resources for home sewing entrepreneurs.

ARTS & CRAFTS BUSINESS AT ABOUT.COM
http://artsandcrafts.about.com

William T. Lasley offers an eclectic mix of links to resources around the Net for craft entrepreneurs, plus articles on topics like where to buy canopies and tents for craft fairs.

Join The Professional Association of Custom Clothiers
Visit their Web site (**http://www.paccprofessionals.org**) for information about this association for sewers who make custom clothing professionally, plus online chats, a news letter, and more.

MAKESTUFF.COM'S ENTREPRENEUR'S CORNER
http://www.makestuff.com/home_business/index.html

Makestuff.Com offers lots of advice on starting a crafty home business. Click on their Craft Resources logo for a directory of craft shows around the country.

GET CREATIVE: CRAFTLINK RESOURCE CENTER
http://www.getcreativeshow.com/Craft_Sew_Business/
craft_business_resource_center.htm

Get Creative offers a selection of articles on starting a home crafting business.

✋ Warning! Beware of E-mail Offers to Make Money by Assembling Crafts at Home

"Would you like to assemble crafts at home and get paid? Be your own boss! Top pay! Earn hundreds of dollars weekly! You can choose from - Beaded Accessories - up to $350.00 Weekly! - Holiday Crafts - up to $270.00 Weekly! - Hair Accessories - up to $320.00 Weekly!" It's one of the most rampant Internet scams. You get an e-mail message promising you hundreds of dollars a week for assembling simple craft items. The catch? You need to buy a craft kit, usually for a hundred dollars or more. Once you assemble the items the company tells you your work is unsatisfactory—but you can keep assembling and sending them more items if you wish. Needless to say, your work is never satisfactory. And the craft items that you're supposed to assemble are so time-intensive, such as beaded hair bands, that no one could ever make a living making and selling them.

Our Favorite Web Resources for Entrepreneurs

Here's a small selection of our favorite general-interest advice sites for entrepreneurs. If you're scoffing that all you do is sew a few dolls each month to sell to friends, just remember: that's how the Cabbage Patch Kids empire started.

YAHOO! SMALL BUSINESS
http://smallbusiness.yahoo.com

An eclectic mix of articles and links to Web resources for entrepreneurs from the Yahoo search site.

INC. ONLINE
http://www.inc.com

The magazine Inc. serves up lots of compelling reading each month, about starting a business and the pitfalls to avoid.

WOMEN CONNECT.COM:
THE SOURCE FOR WOMEN IN BUSINESS
http://www.womenconnect.com

Read features on topics like how to get paperwork done and how to kid-proof your home office.

WHAT'S NOW @ WOW FACTOR.COM
http://www.wowfactor.com

Tap into this resource for women in business to read features and network with others.

CEO EXPRESS!
http://www.ceoexpress.com

CEO Express offers hundreds of links to newspapers, financial magazines, newsfeeds, and more.

free Stuff for Costumers

Hand-in-hand with our conviction that everyone on the Internet is an ardent machine embroiderer is our suspicion that everyone wears a costume. Maybe you dream of promenading down a staircase in Scarlett O'Hara's hoop skirt. Or perhaps you want to slither between the pyramids in your backyard in Cleopatra garb. Maybe you just want to make a cheap pirate costume for your kid for Halloween. Whatever your costuming craving and proclivity there's a Web site out there to help you.

If you're interested in historical costuming consider joining the **Historical Costume Mailing List**. E-mail majordomo@indra.com. In the message type *subscribe H-Costume-digest or subscribe H-Costume.*

If you're not so serious, and if the costumes you stitch are 90 percent acrylic plush, join the footloose faux furriers in the **FURSuit** e-mail discussion group, also known as **The Furry Costume Information Exchange** (**http://www.enteract.com/~rcking/fursuit**). Or if adults dressed as giant pandas scare you, just tap into the **FURSuit FTP** site run by "Fuzzy Tiger."

 ## Halloween Costuming Web Sites

FABRICLINK'S HALLOWEEN COSTUME CLOSET
http://www.fabriclink.com/closet.html

FabricLink offers ideas for economical Halloween costumes.

HALLOWEEN COSTUME MAKING HOW-TOS
http://www.hauntedamerica.com/thehaunted/halloween/
costume/piratecoat.htm

Directions for a pirate coat, prom dress, Grim Reaper costume, and more for the kids.

LATEX MASK MAKING BASICS 🛒
FROM SPECIAL EFFECTS SUPPLY
http://www.xmission.com/~spl_efx/mask/mask.html

HALLOWEEN COSTUME SAFETY FOR KIDS
http://www.kidshealth.org/parent/safety/halloween.html

The Alfred I. duPont Hospital for Children and the National SAFE KIDS Campaign offer a Web page full of tips on making Halloween costumes that are safe for kids.

 General Costuming Web Sites

COSTUMING AND CARE TIPS
http://www.lpl.arizona.edu/~kimberly/medance/suppl/
costumecare.html

This is a great compilation of advice compiled from the Medieval Dance mailing list. Topics include colorfastness and how to clean beads, specialty fabrics, swords, and veils.

HISTORICAL COSTUMING FAQ
http://reality.sgi.com/lara/faq.hist-cost.html

You'll find answers to oft-asked questions on historical costuming patterns and supplies.

DUANE AND KATHRYN'S COSTUME PAGES
http://pages.cthome.net/dkelms/costume.htm

See the beautiful costumes that Duane and Kathryn Elms have stitched, and read some of their essays about costume making, such as the one on choice of color in costuming. Be sure to take a look at the pictures of their Williamsburg costume wedding.

THE COSTUME GALLERY
http://www.costumegallery.com/main.htm

Host to over 400 web pages and 1,800 images of costume.

THE COSTUME PAGE
http://members.aol.com/nebula5/costume.html

This is a great site! Julie Zetterberg offers links to all the best Web resources on costuming, plus lots of information on making costumes and period clothes.

MILIEUX—THE COSTUME SITE
http://milieux.com/costume

Lauren Podolak offers a wonderful directory of costuming resources around the Web for historical and science fiction and other fantasy costuming.

COSTUMING CONSTRUCTION
http://www.qni.com/~wmorris/costume

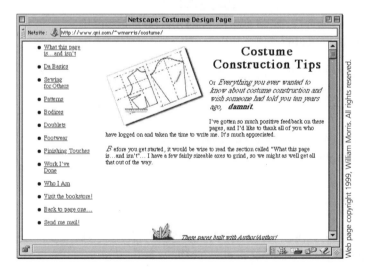

William Richard Morris offers lots of help and opinions on sewing for others, pattern sources, bodices, doublets, footwear, finishing touches and more.

THE PARIS MUSIC HALL COLLECTION
FROM THE HARGRETT LIBRARY,
UNIVERSITY OF GEORGIA
http://scarlett.libs.uga.edu/darchive/hargrett/paris/paris.html

You can browse through over 6,000 original drawings of costume designs and 1,000 original drawings of curtain designs from the music halls of Paris from 1920-1938.

Medieval and Elizabethan Costume Web Sites

THE ELIZABETHAN COSTUME PAGE
http://www.dnaco.net/~aleed/corsets/general.html

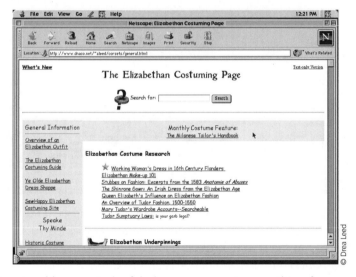

Drea Leed has created a fabulous resource on everything from Elizabethan colors and fabrics to period hats. She even includes a custom corset pattern generator. Insert your measurements and follow step by step instructions for making a corset.

A BEGINNER'S GUIDE TO MEDIEVAL COSTUME BY ANDREW CRAZE & ALAN HOWSHALL

http://www.cf.ac.uk/uwcc/archi/howshall/arthurm/costume/costume.html

ELIZABETHAN PERIOD COSTUMES

http://www.renfaire.com/Costume/costume.html

THE AULD GARB MONGER'S COSTUMES FOR MANLY MEN

http://www.pe.net/~wwweaver/index.html

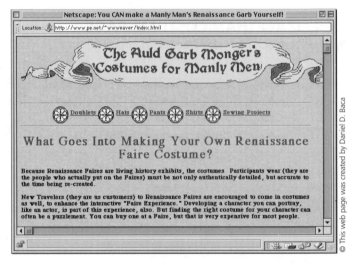

© This web page was created by Daniel D. Baca

First you start by determining whether you want to be a noble-man, a member of the middle-class or a peasant. Then you proceed to the sewing projects and learn how to make manly swashbuckling shirts and doublets and Jerkins and vests.

Colonial and Victorian Costume Web Sites

COSTUMES AND CLOTHING
http://www.wmol.com/whalive/costumes.htm

Sandra Hansen has linked a huge selection of information for putting together period costumes from the American Civil War and later.

THE VICTORIAN FASHION PAGES FROM SHENLEI E. WINKLER
http://www.teasociety.com/victorian/index.html

 Free Basic Costume Patterns

"HOW TO MAKE SIMPLE PANTS" BY DUCHESS LEAH KASMIRA OF NATTERHELM
http://www.unm.edu/~kballar/newcomer/pants.html

"HOW TO MAKE A BASIC T-TUNIC" BY DUCHESS LEAH KASMIRA OF NATTERHELM
http://www.unm.edu/~kballar/newcomer/tunic.html

TEMPUS PEREGRINATOR'S SLEEVES SITE
http://pip1.pipcom.com/~tempus/sleeves/index.html

Learn how to make sleeves from just about any period in history, with patterns as well as historical insights.

COSTUME PATTERNS FROM DAWN DUPERAULT
http://ares.redsword.com/dduperault/patterns.htm

Dawn shares patterns for things like a simple bodice, tunic, pouch, and cloak, plus some advanced patterns.

STAYS, A BRIEF HISTORY AND HOW TO MAKE THEM
http://www.vincents.demon.co.uk/stays/stays.htm

Caroline Vincent explains how to replicate the stiffening techniques used in historic gowns.

free Demos of Pattern-Makin Software—and Help for Using It

Wouldn't it be nice if we could enter our measurements into our home computers, select from different styles of sleeves, bodices, skirts or pants, then sit back as the printer printed a custom pattern? That's the idea behind pattern-making programs. But the software isn't as easy to use as one might think. You need to know how to take and enter the measurements correctly. You need to know enough about pattern drafting to know when the computer has given you a good pattern piece or a bum one. And then you need to know how to stitch up the garment—the software doesn't always give you directions. You need patience, yes, loads of patience. Still, many professional-caliber sewers find it useful at times (especially for making pants).

CAD (computer-aided design) pattern drafting software is an entirely different beast. With this kind of program you actually draw the pattern pieces yourself on the computer screen. The software gives you some help, but again, you better know what you're doing. Professional designers and costumers love these high-end tools. Some even let you create a mannequin in three-dimensions on your computer, then shape the pattern pieces to it.

Quiltropolis (**http://www.quiltropolis.com/NewMailinglists.asp**) hosts several e-mail discussion groups for sewers who use or who are interested in buying one of these programs. **Sewing Only Software**, run by Gail Dennis and Robin Elder, is a support group for all types of sewing software.

Dress Shop Discussions is for sewers who use LivingSoft's popular pattern-generating software and related products.

CAD-PatPro is a by-subscription list for sewers who are drafting patterns using one of the CAD-like programs such as Symmetry, PatternMaker, Fittingly Sew, or one of the general-purpose computer-aided design programs like AutoCad or Corel CAD.

READ JUDY'S REVIEWS OF PATTERN-DRAFTING SOFTWARE IN *SEW NEWS*

You can read Judy's article on the pros and cons of using pattern-drafting software in *Sew News'* **Web site** library (**http://www.sewnews.com/library/fash2.htm**). The software packages she reviewed have changed since this article was published, but it will give you an idea of what it's like to use this software.

Web Sites for Makers of Custom Clothing Pattern-Making Software

Both LivingSoft and Water Fountain Software sell a variety of programs for both PCs and Macs into which you enter your measurements and the software generates a clothing pattern for you. Depending upon which version of these companies' programs that you buy, the custom patterns generated run the gamut from designer suits to children's clothing. Both companies offer various demos and trial versions that you can download from their sites.

🛒 LIVINGSOFT DRESS SHOP
http://www.livingsoft.com/trial.htm

🛒 WATER FOUNTAIN SOFTWARE, INC.
http://www.wfsinc.com/home.html

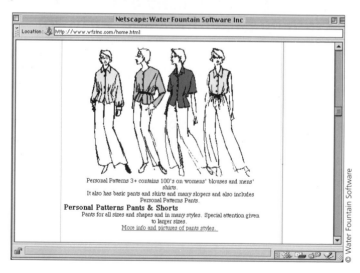

Web Sites for Makers of CAD-Style Pattern-Drafting Software

These companies sell software that allows you to draft garment patterns on your computer screen. They usually come with an assortment of predrawn slopers, and sometimes the companies sell extra garment modules or special versions.

CUSTOM PATTERNMAKER
http://www.access-presto.com/cpminfo

Custom Patternmaker is an add-on to AutoCad that lets you create a three-dimensional body form and fit a pattern too it. No demo is available, but you'll find information on this site. It runs on PCs.

KNITCRAFT FITTINGLY SEW
http://www.knitcraft.com/fittinglysew.html

You can download an excellent demo in Mac or PC flavors.

PATTERNMAKER
http://www.eskimo.com/~pmaker

A CAD-style pattern-drafting program with additional modules for different types of garments. You can download a PC demo.

SYMMETRY FROM
WILD GINGER SOFTWARE, INC.
http://www.wild-ginger.com/symmetry/symtoc.htm

Symmetry is professional-level CAD software for pattern drafting. You can download a PC demo.

 COMPARE FEATURES OF PATTERN MAKING SOFTWARE
Raymond Lowe offers a chart comparing pattern-making programs by price and features
(**http://is2.hk.super.net/~rlowe/sew.html**).

Thinking of Bargain Hunting for Sewing Notions & Patterns In Web Fleamarkets? Read Our Tips First!

Buying vintage sewing patterns, and notions like old buttons and lace on Web fleakmarkets is great fun. Our favorite cyber-fleamarketing spot is **eBay (http://www.ebay.com)**. Through the book we offer special tips for finding sewing goodies for things like bridal sewing, dollmaking, and vintage clothing accessorizing on Web auction sites. But here are some general tips to keep in mind:

- **How safe is buying from Web fleamarkets?** It depends a lot on what you're buying—in our opinion. High-ticket items like consumer electronics are high risk. Remember that in most instance you're not actually buying from the fleamarket but from individuals who advertise on it. Your entire transaction will probably be with a stranger about whom you know nothing but an e-mail address. Judy often buys vintage patterns, beads, and laces on eBay, but rarely buys anything over $10. She frankly isn't too worried that someone who sells old buttons will turn out to be a con artist. She would never buy computer equipment from these sites.

- **Before you bid check the seller's buyer ratings.** Web auction sites let buyers post comments about sellers after a transaction. Although these "buyer ratings" are often not what they're cracked up to be—they can be easily forged, and aggrieved buyers may be too timid to post 'negative feedback'—if a seller boasts hundreds of happy customers that can be a good sign that they will in fact send you your 99 cent buttons without laundering your check.

- **Never send money orders.** Some sellers accept only money orders. If you send a money order you have no way of knowing that your money actually arrived in their hands and they cashed the check.

- **Ask questions before bidding.** Never take anything for granted. If the seller maintains in their description that "all pattern pieces are in tact" ask them how they know. Did they actually take them out of the package and count them? Does the package look opened? Are the instructions in one piece? Does that "Victorian lace" come with a "poly blend" tag? Find out what they plan to charge for shipping.

- **Check the "Ending Today" listings for the best buys.** Most people bid on items in the last hours—or even the last minute before an auction ends. (People who do their bidding in the last minute are called "snipers.")

- **Use the auction site's search engine if you're shopping for something specific.** If you're looking for something particular, like poodle-themed embroidery patterns from the '50s (Judy has a collection of those accumulated from eBay), search the entire auction site for different words, combinations of words, and shortened forms of words, and even misspellings. For instance— poodle, podle, emb., poodle pat.—will all turn up patterns with the proper qualifications. We've found quilt tops accidentally posted with the Rolex watches this way.

- **Save all correspondence with the seller.** Keep the URL of the Web page the item is posted on. And keep in mind, before you bid, that if you get ripped off you'll have little of any recourse.

- **If you're buying a pricey item, use an escrow service.** An escrow service will act as a middle-man in the transaction. You send the check to the escrow service. The seller sends you the item. When you inform the service that you've receive the item satisfactorily, the service forwards your check on to the seller. Some of the online auction sites offer this service for a modest fee.

Judy's Tips for Hunting for Fabric in Web Fleamarkets

Judy's fabric obsessions are slightly different than Gloria's. She loves anything old and faded, and if it has cabbage roses or could be called "vintage," all the better. She loves fabric shopping on Web fleamarkets. Her favorite site is **eBay** (**http://www.ebay.com**).

She uses the main searcher and searches for "fabric" or heads to the Collectibles/ Textiles/Fabric category. This is a great place to hunt for old upholstery fabrics (the stuff someone had in their attic for decades, but never got around to using to reupholster that chair), as well as kitschy curtain fabrics from the '50s and '60s. Printed tea towels and tablecloths from the '50s can also be found in abundance. Judy's favorite find: 20 yards of hot pink pillow ticking from the '70s for $10—enough for a lifetime's worth of "retro" cat beds. Here are her tips for fabric fleamarketing:

Inside the browser window:

eBay item 94899041 [Ends 04/30/99, 07:27:54 PDT] - vintage fabric SPRING GARDEN FLORAL - Netscape

File Edit View Go Communicator Help

Bookmarks   Location: http://cgi.ebay.com/aw-cgi/eBayISAPI.dll?ViewItem&item=94899041   What's Related

vintage fabric SPRING GARDEN FLORAL
JUNGLE FEVER

high quality 1940's cotton .. good weight .. excellent unused condition... selvage to selvage measures 32 1/2"..... each section measures 21 1/2" (64 1/2 " in all) ...beautiful vibrant color.....s/h$4.00

buyer pays shipping and handling. Insurance is recommended for all items and is required on all pottery and items over $100 . new york state residents supply valid resale number or add 7% sales tax. ALL SALES ARE FINAL THIS IS AN AUCTION . PLEASE ASK QUESTIONS BEFORE BIDDING , thank you

thanks for shopping

Document: Done

You can find some great fabric "finds" at Web fleamarkets.

- If the fabric has a print find out how large it is.

- Find out what condition the fabric is in. Does it have any yellowing or fading? Any spots? How about signs of moths? And don't be afraid to ask what it smells like. Does it smell smoky or mildewy or reek of mothballs? Antique dealers in cyberspace are use to "smell" questions.

- Once you get the fabric, clean it thoroughly (put it through the washer twice) and keep it from your other fabric in case it has moths.

- Be sure to ask how much shipping will cost before you bid. The cost of shipping 20 yards of material might make it less of a bargain than you originally thought.

ABOUT THE AUTHORS

Judy Heim

has been an avid needlecrafter for thirty years. She writes a regular column for PC World magazine, and she has written other articles for *Family Circle*, *C/Net*, *Newsweek*, *PC/Computing*, *Cosmopolitan*, and needlework magazines such as *Quilter's Newsletter* and *Sew News*. She is the author of four other books on needlecrafting and the Internet and co-author of the Free Stuff on the Internet Series. Judy lives in Madison, Wisconsin.

Gloria Hansen

has won significant awards for her quilts, most of which were designed using a Macintosh computer. She has written articles for computer magazines (including *Family Circle* and *PC World*) and for quilting magazines (including *Art/Quilt Magazine* and *McCall's Quilting*); she also writes the "High-Tech Quilting" column for The Professional Quilter. She has self-published patterns and her quilts have appeared in numerous magazines, books, and on television. With Judy, she is co-author of *The Quilter's Computer Companion* and co-author of the Free Stuff on the Internet Series. Gloria lives in central New Jersey.

BIBLIOGRAPHY

Heim, Judy and Gloria Hansen, *Free Stuff for Quilters*, C&T Publishing, Concord, CA 1998

._____. *Free Stuff for Quilters, 2nd Edition*, C&T Publishing, Concord, CA 1999

._____. *Free Stuff for Stitchers*, C&T Publishing, Concord, CA 1999

._____. *Free Stuff for Sewing Fanatics*, C&T Publishing, Concord, CA 1999

._____. *The Quilters Computer Companion*, No Starch Press, San Francisco, CA 1998

Heim, Judy, *The Needlecrafter's Companion*, No Starch Press, San Francisco, CA 1999

index

For more information on other fine books from C&T Publishing,
write for a free catalog:
C&T Publishing, Inc.,
P.O. Box 1456, Lafayette, CA 94549
(800) 284-1114
http://www.ctpub.com
e-mail: ctinfo@ctpub.com

FREE STUFF ON THE INTERNET SERIES

Frustrated with spending hours of valuable time surfing your way around the Internet? C&T Publishing's Free Stuff on the Internet Series helps you quickly find information on your favorite craft or hobby. Our Free Stuff guides make it easy to stay organized as you visit hundreds of sites that offer all kinds of free patterns, articles, e-mail advice, galleries, and more. This series of handy guides lets you explore the Internet's infinite possibilities.

Free Stuff for Crafty Kids
Includes Web sites that offer kid-friendly projects, such as craft projects for the whole family, origami, paper airplanes and kites, sewing and other needlecrafts, scrapbook making, rubber stamping, balloon art tutorials, holiday crafts, and cartooning

Free Stuff for Stitchers
Includes Web sites that offer free stuff for all kinds of needlecrafts, including knitting, crochet, embroidery, cross-stitch, tatting, lace-making, and needlepoint. You'll also find how-tos for beading, rugmaking, spinning, weaving, and more

Free Stuff for Quilters, 2nd Edition
The 2nd Edition of *Free Stuff for Quilters* includes over 150 updated new links on quilt patterns and tips, quilt discussion groups, guilds, and organizations, plus quilt shops to visit when you travel, how-tos for fabric dyeing, painting, stamping, photo transferring, and galleries of quilts, textiles, and fiber arts.